DR. ACKERMAN'S BOOK OF THE
DOBERMAN PINSCHER

LOWELL ACKERMAN DVM

BB-107

Overleaf: Doberman Pinschers owned by Linda Hoff.

The author has exerted every effort to ensure that medical information mentioned in this book is in accord with current recommendations and practice at the time of publication. However, in view of the ongoing advances in veterinary medicine, the reader is urged to consult with his veterinarian regarding individual health issues.

Photographers: Beth Bishop, Sheila Bonas, Paulette Braun, P. Butterworth, Isabelle Francais, G. Maxwell, Will and Marion Muirhead, Robin Nuttall, Robert Pearcy, and Robert Smith.

The presentation of pet products in this book is strictly for instructive purposes only; it does not necessarily constitute an endorsement by the author, publisher, owners of dogs portrayed, or any other contributors.

t.f.h.

©1996 by Lowell Ackerman DVM

Distributed in the UNITED STATES to the Pet Trade by T.F.H. Publications, Inc., One T.F.H. Plaza, Neptune City, NJ 07753; distributed in the UNITED STATES to the Bookstore and Library Trade by National Book Network, Inc. 4720 Boston Way, Lanham MD 20706; in CANADA to the Pet Trade by H & L Pet Supplies Inc., 27 Kingston Crescent, Kitchener, Ontario N2B 2T6; Rolf C. Hagen Inc., 3225 Sartelon St. Laurent-Montreal Quebec H4R 1E8; in CANADA to the Book Trade by Vanwell Publishing Ltd., 1 Northrup Crescent, St. Catharines, Ontario L2M 6P5 ; in ENGLAND by T.F.H. Publications, PO Box 15, Waterlooville PO7 6BQ; in AUSTRALIA AND THE SOUTH PACIFIC by T.F.H. (Australia), Pty. Ltd., Box 149, Brookvale 2100 N.S.W., Australia; in NEW ZEALAND by Brooklands Aquarium Ltd. 5 McGiven Drive, New Plymouth, RD1 New Zealand; in Japan by T.F.H. Publications, Japan— Jiro Tsuda, 10-12-3 Ohjidai, Sakura, Chiba 285, Japan; in SOUTH AFRICA by Lopis (Pty) Ltd., P.O. Box 39127, Booysens, 2016, Johannesburg, South Africa. Published by T.F.H. Publications, Inc.
MANUFACTURED IN THE
UNITED STATES OF AMERICA
BY T.F.H. PUBLICATIONS, INC.

CONTENTS

DEDICATION · 4

PREFACE · 4

BIOGRAPHY · 5

BREED HISTORY · 6

MIND & BODY · 10
Conformation and Physical Characteristics · Coat Color, Care, and Condition · Behavior and Personality of the Active Doberman Pinscher

SELECTING THE PERFECT DOBERMAN PINSCHER · 18
Sources · Medical Screening · Behavioral Screening · Organizations You Should Know About

FEEDING & NUTRITION · 28
Commercial Dog Foods · Puppy Requirements · Adult Diets · Geriatric Diets · Medical Conditions and Diet

HEALTH · 36
Two to Three Weeks of Age · Six to Twenty Weeks of Age · Four to Six Months of Age · Six to Twelve Months of Age · The First Seven Years · Senior Dobermans

MEDICAL PROBLEMS · 48
Acral Lick Dermatitis (Lick Granuloma) · Cataracts · Cervical Vertebral Instability (Wobbler Syndrome) · Color Dilution Alopecia · Demodicosis · Dilated Cardiomyopathy · Elbow Dysplasia · Flank Sucking · Gastric Dilatation/Volvulus (Bloat) · Hip Dysplasia · Hypothyroidism · Liver Disease Due to Copper Accumulation · Narcolepsy · Persistent Hyperplastic Primary Vitreous · Sulfa Sensitivity · Von Willebrand's Disease · Other Conditions Seen in the Doberman

INFECTIONS & INFESTATIONS · 68
Fleas · Ticks · Mange · Heartworm · Intestinal Parasites · Viral Infections · Canine Cough

FIRST AID · 78
Temperature · Capillary Refill Time and Gum Color · Heart Rate, Pulse, and Respirations · Preparing for an Emergency · Emergency Muzzle · Antifreeze Poisoning · Bee Stings · Bleeding · Bloat · Burns · Cardiopulmonary Resuscitation (CPR) · Chocolate Toxicosis · Choking · Dog Bites · Drowning · Electrocution · Eyes · Fish Hooks · Foreign Objects · Heatstroke · Poisons · Poisonous Plants · Porcupine Quills · Seizure (Convulsion or Fit) · Severe Trauma · Shock · Skunks · Snake Bites · Toad Poisoning · Vaccination Reaction

RECOMMENDED READING · 95

DEDICATION

To my fantastic wife Susan and my three adorable children, Nadia, Rebecca, and David.

PREFACE

Keeping your Doberman Pinscher healthy is the most important job that you, as an owner, can do. Whereas there are many books available that deal with breed qualities, conformation, and show characteristics, this may be the only book available dedicated entirely to the preventive health care of the Doberman Pinscher. This information has been compiled from a variety of sources and assembled here to provide you with the most up-to-date advice available.

This book will take you through the important stages of selecting your pet, screening it for inherited medical and behavioral problems, meeting its nutritional needs, and seeing that it receives optimal medical care.

So, enjoy the book and use the information to keep your Doberman Pinscher the healthiest it can be for a long, full, and rich life.

Lowell Ackerman DVM

BIOGRAPHY

Dr. Lowell Ackerman is a world-renowned veterinary clinician, author, lecturer and radio personality. He is a Diplomate of the American College of Veterinary Dermatology and is a consultant in the fields of dermatology, nutrition, and genetics. Dr. Ackerman is the author of 34 books and over 150 book chapters and articles. He also hosts a national radio show on pet health care and moderates a site on the World Wide Web dedicated to pet health care issues (http://www.familyinternet.com/pet/pet-vet.htm).

BREED HISTORY

**THE GENESIS OF THE MODERN
DOBERMAN PINSCHER**

The Doberman Pinscher is of relatively recent vintage, being "created" in the late 1800s. The originator, which should come as no surprise, was named Dobermann and the stock which was used to create the breed we know today consisted of German Pinschers and Rottweilers.

Facing page: Some people believe that the rich black and tan markings seen on the Doberman Pinscher were inherited from the Rottweiler, which was among the stock used to create the breed.

In all likelihood, the German Shorthaired Pointer, the Great Dane, the Manchester Terrier, the Beauceron, the Weimaraner, and cattle-driving dogs also participated in those early breedings. The first stud book registration took place in 1893 and the breed became progressively more popular. The first Doberman Pinscher came to the United States around 1908.

World War I took its toll on the Doberman breeders and many dogs died from malnutrition or were shipped overseas following armistice. Less fortunate animals were actually eaten by dognappers or killed because there was no food to feed them. Clearly, it was the lucky ones that managed to leave the country. In fact, by the end of the war, most of the best quality Dobermans of Europe had been sold to owners in the United States. The breed recovered nicely in Germany over the next two decades when many were pressed into military service.

The cropped ears and docked tails of the modern Doberman Pinscher are much different than those of the early Doberman. The ears were cropped short and the tails were more bobbed than docked. Owners, Grace and Raquel Acosta.

The early Dobermans were significantly different from those of today. Their ears were cropped extremely short so that they couldn't be grabbed by adversaries. Aggressiveness was very desirable in those days and the dogs were much "harder" than the housepets of today. In those days, aggressiveness was a trait to be encouraged. Today, aggressiveness is not a desirable trait and has no place in a dog living in a family environment.

The early Dobermans also had more "bobbed" than "docked" tails. Early reports suggest that many litters were produced in which the dogs only had stubs for tails. However, breedings failed to produce "lines" of bobbed Dobermans and docking became a common procedure.

After World War II, the Doberman breed became even more popular. By 1970, they ranked 14th in American Kennel Club registrations. In 1994, they were the 18th most commonly registered breed with the American Kennel Club. This is very impressive for a breed that was created less than a century before.

Whereas the Doberman originated as a guard dog, the breed of today is considerably more versatile. Dobermans can be ex-

Although the Doberman Pinscher can still be trained as a guard dog, today the breed has become much more versatile. More and more owners are socializing their Dobermans as house pets rather than as guard dogs.

cellent hunters, trackers, and herding dogs as well as service dogs for the blind, deaf, and infirmed. Above all, Doberman Pinschers continue to be working dogs and are happiest when they are recognized as such. It is encouraging to see that now that Doberman Pinschers have outgrown their aggressive mode, more and more owners are socializing them as housepets rather than as guard dogs. There is also an international movement to stop cosmetically altering the tails and ears of the breed. These are steps in the right direction.

MIND & BODY

**PHYSICAL AND BEHAVIORAL TRAITS
OF THE DOBERMAN PINSCHER**

A working dog through and through, the Doberman Pinscher is a loyal and obedient watchdog and companion. He is a dog of fearless character, ever alert and determined. Most importantly, the Doberman is neither shy nor aggressive. The breed's elegant appearance is in harmony with his noble disposition and proud carriage.

Facing page: The Doberman Pinscher is alert, intelligent, beautiful, and strong. All of these qualities combined make him both a loving companion and a faithful guardian. Owner, Carol Petruzzo.

While each dog must be treated as an individual, the true Doberman must demonstrate all these positive characteristics.

CONFORMATION AND PHYSICAL CHARACTERISTICS

This is not a book about show dogs, so information here will not deal with the conformation of champions and how to select one. The purpose of this chapter is to provide basic information about the stature of a Doberman Pinscher and qualities of a physical nature.

Beauty is clearly in the eye of the beholder. Since standards come and standards go, measuring your dog against some imaginary yardstick does little for you or your dog. Just because your dog isn't a show champion doesn't mean that he or she is any less of a family member, likewise, just because a dog is a champion doesn't mean that he or she is not a genetic time bomb waiting to go off.

When breeders and those interested in showing Dobermans select their dogs, they look for those qualities that match the breed "standard." This standard, however, is of an imaginary Doberman and it changes from time to time and from country to country. Thus, the conformation and physical characteristics that pet owners should concentrate

Doberman Pinschers are medium-sized dogs. Their bodies are square, compactly built, and muscular.

It is not necessary to have your Doberman Pinscher's ears cropped. As a matter of fact, it is illegal in England, Australia, and a number of other countries. Should you prefer natural ears, inform the breeder right away.

on are somewhat different and much more practical.

Dobermans were originally bred to be small- to medium-sized dogs but, as they were used for more and more guard work, they were bred to become progressively larger. Most adult males are 27–28 inches at the withers and bitches are about 2 inches smaller. The normal weight range for the breed is 66–88 pounds (30–40 kg) but a better target is about 70 pounds for females and 75 pounds for males. Larger dogs are not nec-

essarily better dogs. Doberman Pinschers were never intended to be considered "giants" and the increased size might promote some medical problems which tend to be more common in larger dogs. There is some preliminary evidence that the larger members of the breed might not only be more susceptible to orthopedic disorders such as elbow dysplasia and hip dysplasia but also to heart ailments such as dilated cardiomyopathy. DNA testing is currently being researched and should help answer these and other questions related to size and genetic passage of medical problems.

Doberman puppies have floppy houndlike ears and lovely tails unless there is surgical intervention. Be aware that it is not necessary to either crop the ears or dock the tails in the Doberman for it to be a purebred. Being a true Doberman has to do with genetics, not surgery. For those wanting to indulge, tails and dewclaws tend to be docked when pups are three days old; ears are most often cropped at about six to eight weeks of age. Most veterinary associations and even many breed registries are against altering animals to create an artificial image. Consider carefully your rationale if you decide to have these procedures done.

COAT COLOR, CARE, AND CONDITION

There are four "approved" colors of the Doberman Pinscher: black, red, blue, and fawn (Isabella). All Dobermans have short coats and are easy to groom. A moisturizing shampoo and conditioner are often needed because the breed has a tendency toward dry skin and coat. Pubescent dogs, usually males, also have a tendency to develop chin acne and medi-

cated shampoos, scrubs, and gels are usually necessary.

The normal undiluted colors for Dobermans are black (and tan) and red. The blues and fawns are suitable only for enthusiasts; they have frequent skin and coat problems. In fact, it is rare to see blue and fawn Dobermans with full coats by six years of age although the coat always appears completely normal in pups and young dogs. The condition is known as color dilution alopecia or color "mutant" alopecia because the dilution gene "d," which is responsible for the interesting color, is also responsible for the eventual hair loss (alopecia). The defective hair follicles eventually stop making normal hairs and the result is considerable time and expense with specialists, nutritional supplements, and skin treatments for an incurable disorder. Take this advice..."don't be a pawn—forget blue and fawn."

The genetics of coat color are fairly simple in the Doberman and are controlled by two different genes. One gene determines if the base color is black or red (with black being dominant) and the other determines whether or not the color is diluted or undiluted (with undiluted being dominant). Diluted "blacks" become "blues" and diluted "reds" become "fawns."

Without becoming geneticists we can still appreciate how the colors occur in the breed with some basic rules. Each pup receives half of its genes from its mother and half from its father. Black is the dominant trait, referred to by the capital letter "B." A small "b" signifies red but is recessive; it takes two (bb) for the dog to be red in color. Since black is the dominant color, a dog will be black with either two (BB) or one (Bb) black genes. Dogs will only be red if they have both recessive genes (bb). One important point here—you can't tell if a dog is BB or Bb by looking; they're both black! This demonstrates the difference between genotype and phenotype. Genotype refers to the genetic combinations which we can't see (e.g., BB, Bb, bb) while phenotype refers to the products which we can see (e.g., black, red). If a mating of black Dobermans produces any red pups, you can infer that both parents had to be carriers (Bb) since a recessive gene must have been inherited from each parent. And, if you breed a red Doberman (bb) to any black Doberman (BB or Bb), all the offspring will be either black carriers (Bb) or reds (bb).

What about blues and fawns?

Fawn (Isabella) is a color of the Doberman Pinscher that is a diluted version of the red color seen in the breed. Both colors are shown here.

Well, the genetics are identical. Not only do parents pass either a "B" or "b" to their pups, they do the same with the dilution gene "D." The undiluted colors (blacks and reds) are dominant (D) to the diluted colors (blues and fawns) which are recessive (d). Dogs that carry the genes DD and Dd are undiluted while those with "dd" are diluted. Thus, a black Doberman (BB or Bb) will be black if it also carries the genes DD or Dd. With two diluted genes (dd), we have a blue Doberman. Red Dobermans

Coloring of the Doberman Pinscher is a matter of genetics. Depending on the color of the parents, puppies can be black, red, blue, or fawn (Isabella). Owner, Marion Muirhead.

BEHAVIOR AND PERSONALITY OF THE ACTIVE DOBERMAN PINSCHER

Behavior and personality are two qualities which are hard to standardize within a breed. The Doberman Pinscher Club of America, in its standard, looks for dogs to be energetic, watchful, determined, alert, fearless, loyal, and obedient without being shy or vicious. These are all valued traits in any breed.

Although generalizations are difficult to make, most Doberman Pinschers are alert and people-oriented. They make great working dogs because they have the capacity to be loyal, determined, watchful, and obedient. However, it is their social nature that makes them want to work with people. This is not the breed to be tied in the backyard to serve as a watchdog. Whether the dogs are shy or vicious has something to do with their genetics, but is also determined by the socialization and training they receive.

(bb) remain red with DD or Dd; when they are bbdd, they are fawn in color. Fawn Dobermans carry both recessive genes and, on breeding, two fawn Dobermans should produce only fawn Dobermans.

Here are the combinations that give us our Doberman colors:

Phenotype (Color)	Genotype (Actual genetic pairing)			
Black	BBDD	BbDD	BBDd	BbDd
Blue	BBdd	Bbdd		
Red	bbDD	bbDd		
Fawn	bbdd			

Behavior and personality are incredibly important in dogs and there seem to be quite evident extremes in the Doberman Pinscher. The earliest of the breed were bred for aggression and that didn't make them ideal house pets. They were working dogs. Today's Doberman Pinschers seem far removed from their earliest ancestors. In fact, some complain that their Doberman is overly shy and fearful—a wimp. Doberman Pinschers also seem to be overrepresented in behavior clinics, not for aggression, but for neurotic and compulsive behaviors. The ideal Doberman is neither aggressive nor neurotic but rather a loving family member with good self-esteem and acceptance of its position in the family "pack." Because the Doberman Pinscher is a powerful dog and can cause much damage, it is worth spending the time when selecting a pup to pay attention to any evidence of personality problems. It is also imperative that *all* Doberman Pinschers be obedience trained. Like any dog, they have the potential to be vicious without appropriate training; consider obedience classes mandatory for your sake and for that of your dog.

Although many Dobermans are happy to sleep the day away in bed or on a sofa, most enjoy having a purpose in their day and that makes them excellent working dogs. They do not need long daily walks but they do appreciate events that involve family members. Do not let Doberman pups run unrestricted because it can increase their risk of developing orthopedic disorders. All Doberman Pinschers should attend obedience classes, and they need to learn limits to unacceptable behaviors. A well-loved and well-controlled Doberman is certain to be a valued family member.

For pet owners, there are several activities to which your Doberman is well-suited. Doberman Pinschers not only make great walking and jogging partners but they are also excellent community volunteers. Many services enlist Dobermans and their owners to visit hospitals, homes for the aged, and shut-ins. The loyal and intelligent Doberman will be your personal guard dog if properly trained; aggressiveness and viciousness do not fit into the equation.

For Doberman enthusiasts who want to get into more competitive aspects of the dog world, showing, obedience, hunting, guarding, tracking, herding, and Schutzhund are all activities that can be considered.

SELECTING

**WHAT YOU NEED TO KNOW TO FIND
THE BEST DOBERMAN PUPPY**

Owning the perfect Doberman rarely happens by accident. On the other hand, owning a genetic dud is almost always the result of an

impulsive purchase and failure to do basic research. Buying this book is a major step in understanding the situation and making intelligent choices.

Facing page: Owning the perfect Doberman can be achieved only with time, research, and careful consideration. Don't ever buy a puppy on impulse.

SOURCES

Recently, a survey was done to determine whether there were more problems seen in animals adopted from pet stores, breeders, private owners, or animal shelters. Somewhat surprisingly, there didn't appear to be any major difference in total number of problems seen from these sources. What was different were the kinds of problems seen in each source. Thus, you can't rely on any one source because there are no standards by which judgments can be made. Most veteri-narians will recommend that you select a "good breeder" but there is no way to identify such an individual. A breeder of champion show dogs may also be a breeder of genetic defects. Also, to save yourself grief and expense later, avoid fads such as the blue and fawn Dobermans. They may look exotic, but in most cases, they will present you with too many skin problems to be worthwhile.

The best approach is to select a pup from a source that regularly performs genetic screening

When selecting a Doberman puppy strictly as a pet, concentrate on the things that are important. A mark here or there that may detract from the show dog will not affect its ability to be a loving and healthy pet.

Doberman puppies have floppy hound-like ears. Ears are most often cropped around six to eight weeks of age, if desired.

and has documentation to prove it. If you are intending to be a pet owner, don't worry about whether your pup is of show quality. A mark here or there that might disqualify the pup as a show winner has absolutely no impact on its ability to be a loving and healthy pet. Also, the vast majority of dogs will be neutered and not used for breeding anyway. Concentrate on the things that are important.

MEDICAL SCREENING

Whether you are dealing with a breeder, a breed rescue group, a shelter, or a pet store, your approach should be the same. You want to identify a Doberman that you can live with and screen it for medical and behavioral problems before you make

it a permanent family member. If the source you select has not done the important testing needed, make sure they will offer you a health/temperament guarantee before you remove the dog from the premises to have the work done yourself. If this is not acceptable, or they are offering an exchange-only policy, keep moving; this isn't the right place for you to get a dog. As soon as you purchase a Doberman, pup or adult, go to your veterinarian for a thorough evaluation and testing.

Pedigree analysis is best left to true enthusiasts but there are some things that you can do, even as a novice. Inbreeding is to be discouraged, so check out your four or five generation pedigree and look for names that appear repeatedly. Most breeders linebreed, which is acceptable, so you may see the same *prefix* many times but not the same actual dog or bitch. Reputable breeders will usually not allow inbreeding at least three generations back in the puppy's pedigree. Also ask the breeder to provide OFA and CERF registration numbers on all ancestors in the pedigree for which testing is done. If there are a lot of gaps, the breeder has some explaining to do.

The screening procedure is easier if you select an older dog. Animals can be registered for hips and elbows as young as two years of age by the Orthopedic Foundation for Animals (OFA) and by one year of age by Genetic Disease Control (GDC). This is your insurance against hip dysplasia and elbow dysplasia later in life. Although Doberman Pinschers now have a relatively low incidence of these orthopedic problems, it is due to the efforts of conscientious breeders who have been doing the appropriate testing. A verbal testimonial that they've never heard of the condition in their lines is not adequate and probably means that they really don't know if they have a problem. Move along.

Evaluation is somewhat more complicated in the Doberman puppy. The PennHip™ procedure can determine risk for developing hip dysplasia in pups as young as 16 weeks of age. For pups younger than that, you should request copies of OFA or GDC registration for both parents. If the parents haven't both been registered, their hip and elbow status should be considered unknown and questionable.

All Doberman Pinschers, regardless of age, should be screened for evidence of von Willebrand's disease. This can be accomplished with a simple blood test. The incidence of this disease is so high in the breed that there is no excuse for not performing the test.

For animals older than one year of age, your veterinarian will also want to take a blood sample to check for thyroid function and liver disease in addition to von Willebrand's disease. All are common in the Doberman Pinscher. A heartworm test, urinalysis, and evaluation of feces for internal parasites should also be done. If there are any patches of hair loss, a skin scraping should be taken to determine if the dog has evidence of demodectic mange.

Your veterinarian should also perform a very thorough

If you select an older Doberman Pinscher, the screening process is much easier than that of a puppy, and you have a better chance of getting a healthy animal.

ophthalmologic (eye) examination. The most common eye problems in Doberman Pinschers are cataracts, persistent pupillary membranes, and retinal dysplasia. It is best to acquire a pup whose parents have both been screened for heritable eye diseases and certified "clear" by organizations such as the Canine Eye Registration Foundation (CERF). If this has been the case, an examination by your veterinarian is probably sufficient and referral to an ophthalmologist is only necessary if recommended by your veterinarian.

As soon as you bring your new Doberman home, whether he is an adult or a puppy, bring him to the veterinarian for medical and behavioral screening. Owner, Stacy C. Perry.

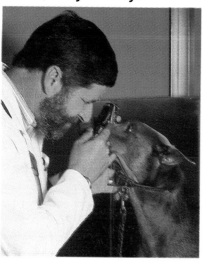

BEHAVIORAL SCREENING

Medical screening is important, but don't forget temperament. More dogs are killed each year for behavioral reasons than for all medical problems combined. Temperament testing is a valuable although not infallible tool in the screening process. The reason that temperament is so important is that many dogs are eventually destroyed because they exhibit undesirable behaviors. Although not all behaviors are evident in young pups (e.g., aggression often takes many months to manifest itself), detecting anxious and fearful pups (and avoiding them) can be very important in the selection process. Traits most identifiable in the young pup include fear, excitability, low pain threshold, extreme submission, and noise sensitivity.

Pups can be evaluated for temperament as early as seven to eight weeks of age. Some behaviorists, breeders, and trainers recommend objective testing where scores are given in several different categories. Others are more casual about the process since it is only a crude indicator. In general, the evaluation takes place in three stages and is conducted by someone the pup has not been exposed to. The testing is not done within 72 hours of

This shy little pup is hiding under the bed. Temperament tests are helpful in determining which puppies are more outgoing than others and vice-versa. Owner, Nanci Kelley.

vaccination or surgery. First, the pup is observed and handled to determine its sociability. Puppies with obvious undesirable traits such as shyness, overactivity, or uncontrollable biting may turn out to be unsuitable. Second, the desired pup is separated from the others and observed for how it responds when played with and called. Third, the pup should be stimulated in various ways and its responses noted. Suitable activities include lying the pup on its side, grooming it, clipping its nails, gently grasping it around the muzzle, and testing its reactions to noise. In a study conducted at the Psychology Department of Colorado State University, it was also found that heart rate is a good indicator in this third stage of evaluation. Actually, they noted the pups' resting heart rates, stimulated the pups with a loud noise, and measured how long it took their heart rates to recover to resting levels. Most pups recovered within 36 seconds. Dogs that took considerably longer were more likely to be anxious.

Puppy Aptitude Tests (PAT) can be given in which a numerical score is given for eleven different traits, with a "1" representing the most assertive or aggressive expression of a trait and a "6" representing disinterest, independence, or inaction. The traits assessed in the PAT include social attraction to people, following, restraint, social dominance, elevation (lifting off ground by evaluator), retrieving, touch sensitivity, sound sensitivity, prey/chase drive, stability, and energy level. Although the tests do not absolutely predict behaviors, they tend to do well at predicting puppies with behavioral extremes.

ORGANIZATIONS YOU SHOULD KNOW ABOUT

Project TEACH™ (Training and Education in Animal Care and Health) is a voluntary accreditation process for those individuals selling animals to the public. It is administered by Pet Health Initiative, Inc. (PHI) and provides instruction on genetic screening as well as many other aspects of proper pet care. TEACH-accredited sources screen animals for a variety of medical, behavioral, and infectious diseases *before* they are sold. Project TEACH™ supports the efforts of registries such as OFA, GDC, and CERF, and recommends that all animals sold be registered with the appropriate agencies. For more information on Project TEACH™, send a self-addressed stamped envelope to Pet Health Initiative, P.O. Box 12093, Scottsdale, AZ 85267-2093.

The Orthopedic Foundation for Animals (OFA) is a nonprofit organization established in 1966 to collect and disseminate information concerning orthopedic diseases of animals and to establish control programs to lower the incidence of these diseases. A registry is maintained for both hip dysplasia and elbow dysplasia. The ultimate purpose of OFA certification is to provide information to dog owners to assist in the selection of good breeding animals; therefore, attempts to get a dysplastic dog certified will only hurt the breed by perpetuation of the disease. For more information, contact your veterinarian or the Orthopedic Foundation for Animals, 2300 Nifong Blvd., Columbia, MO 65201,.

The Institute for Genetic Disease Control in Animals (GDC) is a nonprofit organization founded in 1990 which maintains an open registry for orthopedic problems but does not compete with OFA. In an open regis-

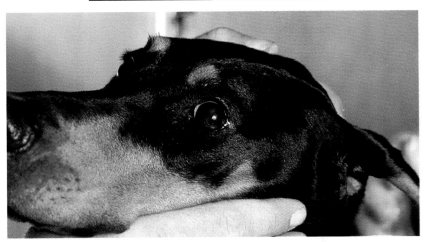

The Canine Eye Registration Foundation certifies purebred dogs as free of hereditary eye diseases. Any Doberman used for breeding should be evaluated by a veterinary eye specialist.

try like GDC, owners, breeders, veterinarians, and scientists can trace the genetic history of any particular dog once that dog and close relatives have been registered. At the present time, GDC operates open registries for hip dysplasia, elbow dysplasia, and osteochondrosis. GDC is currently developing guidelines for registries of Legg-Calve-Perthes disease, craniomandibular osteopathy, and medial patellar luxation. Of these, only craniomandibular osteopathy is significant in the Doberman Pinscher. For more information, contact the Institute for Genetic Disease Control in Animals, P.O. Box 222, Davis, CA 95617.

The Canine Eye Registration Foundation (CERF) is an inter-national organization devoted to eliminating hereditary eye diseases from purebred dogs. CERF is a non-profit organization that screens and certifies purebreds as free of heritable eye diseases. Dogs are evaluated by veterinary eye specialists and the findings are then submitted to CERF for documentation. The goal is to identify purebreds without heritable eye problems so they can be used for breeding. Dogs being considered for breeding programs should be screened and certified by CERF on an annual basis since not all problems are evident in puppies. For more information on CERF, write to CERF, SCC-A, Purdue University, West Lafayette, IN 47907.

FEEDING & NUTRITION

WHAT YOU MUST CONSIDER EVERY DAY TO FEED YOUR DOBERMAN PINSCHER THROUGH HIS LIFETIME

N utrition is one of the most important aspects of raising a healthy Doberman Pinscher and yet it is often the source of much controversy between breeders, veterinarians, pet owners, and dog food manufacturers. However, most of these arguments have more to do with marketing than with science.

Facing page: Ideally, you want to choose a diet for your Doberman Pinscher that meets his needs, is economical, and causes no apparent problems.

Let's first take a look at dog foods and then determine the needs of our dog. This chapter will concentrate of feeding the pet Doberman Pinscher rather than breeding or working animals.

COMMERCIAL DOG FOODS

Most dog foods are sold based on marketing (i.e., how to make a product appealing to owners while meeting the needs of dogs). Some foods are marketed on the

By two months of age Doberman puppies should be fed puppy food, as they are in an important growth phase and nutritional deficiencies at this time can be devastating.

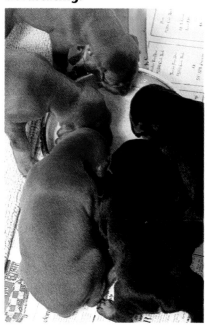

basis of protein content, others are based on a "special" ingredient, and others are sold because they don't contain certain ingredients (e.g., preservatives, soy). We want a dog food that specifically meets our dog's needs, is economical, and causes few, if any, problems. Most foods come in dry, semi-moist, and canned forms. Some can now be purchased frozen. The "dry" foods are the most economical, contain the least fat, and the most preservatives. The canned foods are the most expensive (they're 75% water), usually contain the most fat, and have the least preservatives. Semi-moist foods are expensive and high in sugar content, and I do not recommend them for any dogs.

When you're selecting a commercial diet, make sure the food has been assessed by feeding trials for a specific life stage, not just by nutrient analysis. This statement is usually located not far from the ingredient label. In the United States, these trials are performed in accordance with the American Association of Feed Control Officials (AAFCO) and, in Canada, by the Canadian Veterinary Medical Association. This certification is important because it has been found that dog foods currently on the market that provide only chemical

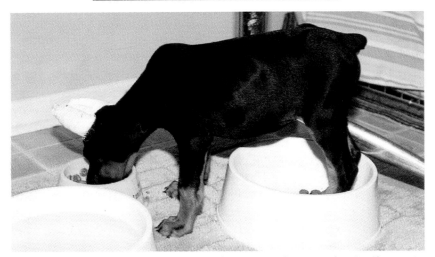

This Doberman puppy wasn't getting enough to eat in the litter. At four weeks of age, she has gained some weight but you can still see her hip bones.

analyses and calculated values, but no feeding trials, may not provide adequate nutrition. The feeding trials show that the diets meet minimal, not optimal, standards. However, they are the best tests we currently have.

PUPPY REQUIREMENTS

Soon after pups are born, and certainly within their first 24 hours, they should begin nursing from their mother. This provides them with colostrum, which is an antibody-rich milk that helps protect them from infection for their first few months of life. Pups should be allowed to nurse for at least six weeks before they are completely weaned from their mother. Supplemen-

tal feeding may be started by as early as three weeks of age.

By two months of age, pups should be fed puppy food. They are now in an important growth phase. Nutritional deficiencies and/or imbalances during this time of life are more devastating than at any other time. Also, this is not the time to overfeed pups or to provide them with "performance" rations. Overfeeding Dobermans can lead to serious skeletal defects such as osteochondrosis, cervical vertebral instability, and hip dysplasia.

Pups should be fed "growth" diets until they are 12–18 months of age. Many Doberman Pinschers do not mature until 18 months of age, and therefore benefit from longer periods on these rations. Pups will initially need to be fed two to three meals daily until they are 12–18 months old, then once to twice daily (preferably twice) when they are converted to adult food. Proper growth diets should be selected based on acceptable feeding trials designed for growing pups. If you can't tell by reading the label, ask your veterinarian for feeding advice.

Remember that pups need balance in their diets and avoid the temptation to supplement with protein, vitamins, or minerals. Calcium supplements have been implicated as a cause of bone and cartilage deformity, especially in large-breed puppies. Puppy diets are already heavily fortified with calcium, and supplements tend to unbalance the mineral intake. There is more than adequate proof that these supplements are responsible for many bone deformities seen in growing dogs.

ADULT DIETS

The goal of feeding adult dogs is one of maintenance. They have already done all the growing they are going to do and are unlikely to have the digestive problems of elderly dogs. In general, dogs can do well on maintenance ra-

tions containing predominantly plant- or animal-based ingredients as long as the rations have been specifically formulated to meet maintenance level requirements. This contention should be supported by studies performed by the manufacturer in accordance with AAFCO (American Association of Feed Control Officials). In Canada, these products should be certified by the Canadian Veterinary Medical Association to meet maintenance requirements.

There's nothing wrong with feeding a cereal-based diet to dogs on maintenance rations and they are the most economical. Soy is a common ingredient in cereal-based diets, but may not be completely digested by all dogs, especially Dobermans. This causes no medical problems, although Dobermans may tend to be more flatulent on these diets. When comparing maintenance rations, it must be appreciated that these diets must meet the minimal requirements for confined dogs, not necessarily optimal levels. Most dogs will benefit when fed diets containing easily digested ingredients that provide nutrients at least slightly above minimum requirements. Typically, these foods will be intermediate in price between the most expensive super-premium diets and the cheapest generic diets. Select only those diets that have been substantiated by feeding trials to meet maintenance requirements, those that contain wholesome ingredients, and those recommended by your veterinarian. Don't select based on price, company advertising, or total protein content.

GERIATRIC DIETS

Doberman Pinschers are considered elderly when they are about seven years of age, and there are certain changes that occur as dogs age that alter their nutritional requirements. As pets age, their metabolism slows and this must be accounted for. If maintenance rations are fed in the same amounts while metabolism is slowing, weight gain may result. Obesity is the last thing one wants to contend with in an elderly pet, since it increases the risk of several other health-related problems. As pets age, most of their organs do not function as well as they did in youth. The digestive system, the liver, the pancreas, and the gallbladder are not functioning at peak effect. The intestines have more difficulty extracting all the nutrients from the food consumed. A gradual decline in kidney function is considered a normal part of aging.

A responsible approach to geriatric nutrition is to realize that degenerative changes are a normal part of aging. Our goal is to minimize the potential damage by taking this into account while the dog is still well. If we wait until an elderly dog is ill before we change the diet, we have a much harder job.

Elderly dogs need to be treated as individuals. While some benefit from the nutrition found in "senior" diets, others might do better on the highly-digestible puppy and super-premium diets. These latter diets provide an excellent blend of digestibility and amino acid content but, unfortunately, many contain more salt and phosphorus than the older pet really needs.

Older dogs are also more prone to developing arthritis, and therefore, it is important not to overfeed them since obesity puts added stress on the joints. For animals with joint pain, supplementing their diets with fatty acid combinations containing cis-linoleic acid, gamma-linolenic acid, and eicosapentaenoic acid can be quite beneficial.

MEDICAL CONDITIONS AND DIET

It is important to keep in mind that dietary choices can affect the development of orthopedic diseases such as hip dysplasia, cervical vertebral instability, and osteochondrosis. When feeding a pup at risk, avoid high-calorie diets and try to feed several times a day rather than ad libitum. Sudden growth spurts can result in joint instability. Recent research has also suggested that the electrolyte balance of the diet may also play a role in the development of hip dysplasia. Rations that had more balance between the positively and negatively charged elements in the diet (e.g., sodium, potassium, chloride) were less likely to promote hip dysplasia in susceptible dogs. Avoid supplements of calcium, phosphorus, and vitamin D as they can interfere with normal bone and cartilage development. The fact is that calcium levels in the body are carefully regulated by hormones (such as calcitonin and parathormone) as well as vitamin D. Supplementation disturbs this normal regulation and can cause many problems. It has also been shown that calcium supplementation can interfere with the proper absorption of zinc from the intestines. If you really feel the need to supplement your dog's diet, select products such as eicosapentaenoic/gamma-linolenic fatty acid combinations or small amounts of vitamin C.

You can't prevent heart disease in dogs entirely by dietary changes, but there are some things that you can do to help. In addition to selecting a properly formulated diet, nutritional supplements can be a useful addition in this case. Some breeds prone to dilated cardiomyopathy have been shown to respond to supplements of L-carnitine, taurine, and/or coenzyme Q. Although Doberman Pinschers are the breed afflicted most commonly with this disorder, a nutritional link has not been determined in this breed. Until the research has been done, it may be advisable to begin supplementation with coenzyme Q10 by two years of age. A dose has not been precisely determined for dogs, but some cardiologists are using doses of 30–90 mg/day. The soft gelatin capsules are preferred and they can be orally administered or punctured and squirted onto the food. This has been shown to improve heart muscle function and may delay the onset of clinical heart disease in susceptible animals.

Diet can't prevent bloat (gastric dilatation/volvulus) but changing feeding habits can make a difference. Initially, the bloat occurs when the stomach becomes distended with swallowed air. This air is swallowed as a consequence of gulping food or water, stress, and/or exercising to close to mealtime. This is where we can make a difference. Divide meals and feed the dog three times daily rather than all at once. Soak dry dog food in water before feeding to decrease the dog's tendency to gulp the food. If you want to feed dry food only, add some large clean chew toys to the feed bowl so that the dog has to "pick" to get at the food and can't gulp it. Putting the food bowl on a step-stool so the dog doesn't have to stretch to get the food may also be helpful. Finally, don't allow any exercise for at least one hour before and after feeding.

Fat supplements are probably the most common supplements purchased from pet supply stores. They frequently promise to add luster, gloss, and sheen to the coat, and consequently, make dogs look healthy. The only fatty acid that is essential for this purpose is cis-linoleic acid, which is found in flaxseed oil, sunflower seed oil, and safflower oil. Corn oil is a suitable but less effective alternative. Most of the other oils found in retail supplements are high in saturated and monounsaturated fats and are not beneficial for shiny fur or healthy skin. For dogs with aller-

gies, arthritis, high blood pressure (hypertension), high cholesterol, and some heart ailments, other fatty acids may be prescribed by a veterinarian. The important ingredients in these products are gamma-linolenic acid (GLA), eicosapentaenoic acid (EPA), and docosahexaenoic acid (DHA). These products have gentle and natural anti-inflammatory properties. But don't be fooled by imitations. Most retail fatty acid supplements do not contain these functional forms of the essential fatty acids—look for gamma-linolenic acid, eicosapentaenoic acid, and docosahexaenoic acid on the label.

Zinc is an important mineral when it comes to immune function and wound healing, but it has some other uses in the Doberman. Zinc administration, particularly zinc acetate, can also promote copper excretion from the body. Usually this is not necessary or even desirable, but some Doberman Pinschers have an inherited disease that causes them to store copper in their livers; the result can be chronic hepatitis. Although this copper-induced hepatitis cannot be cured, zinc supplementation can be used as a safe and effective form of therapy.

HEALTH

**PREVENTIVE MEDICINE AND HEALTH CARE
FOR YOUR DOBERMAN PINSCHER**

Keeping your Doberman Pinscher healthy requires preventive health care. This is not only the most effective but also the least expensive way to battle illness.

Good preventive care starts even before puppies are born. The dam should be well cared for, vaccinated, and free of infections and parasites.

Facing page: Your Doberman's annual veterinary visit is a good opportunity for a thorough physical examination. The examination should include listening to the heart and lungs.

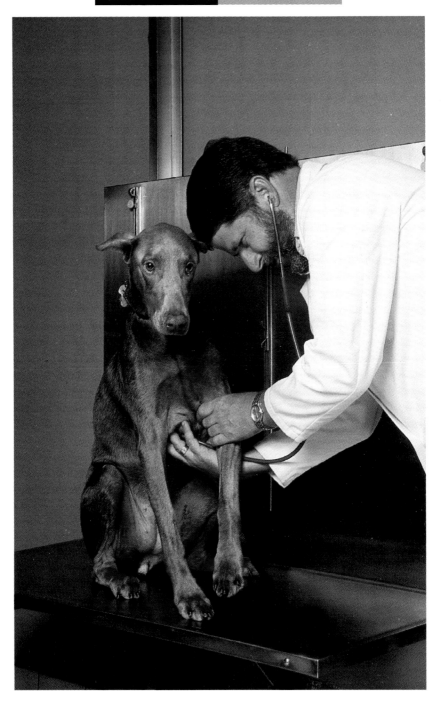

Your Doberman puppy will have a good start in life if his parents were properly screened and found to be good breeding candidates. Owner, Carol Kepler.

Hopefully, both parents were screened for important genetic diseases (e.g. von Willebrands's disease), were registered with the appropriate agencies (e.g., OFA, GDC, CERF), showed no evidence of medical or behavioral problems, and were found to be good candidates for breeding. This gives the pup a good start in life. If all has been planned well, the dam will pass on to her pups a resistance to disease that will last for their first few months of life. However, the dam can also pass on parasites, infections, genetic diseases, and more.

TWO TO THREE WEEKS OF AGE

By two to three weeks of life, it is usually necessary to start pups on a regimen to control worms. Although dogs benefit from parasite control, the primary reason for doing this is human health. After whelping, the dam often sheds large numbers of worms even if she has previously tested negative. This is because many worms lay dormant in tissues and the stress of delivery causes the parasites to be released and shed into the environment. Assume that all puppies potentially have worms because studies have shown that 75% of them do. Thus, we institute worm control early to protect the people in the house from worms, more than the pups themselves. The deworming is repeated every two to three weeks until your veterinarian feels the condition is under control. Nursing bitches should be treated because they often shed worms during this time. Only use products recommended by your veterinarian. Over-the-counter parasiticides have been responsible for deaths in pups.

SIX TO TWENTY WEEKS OF AGE

Most puppies are weaned from their mother at six to eight weeks of age. Weaning shouldn't be done too early so that the pups have the opportunity to socialize with their littermates and dam. This is important for them to be able to interact with other dogs later in life. There is no reason to rush the weaning process unless the dam can't produce enough milk to feed the pups.

Pups are usually first examined by the veterinarian at six to eight weeks of age, which is when most vaccination schedules commence. If pups are exposed to many other dogs at this young age, veterinarians often opt for vaccinating with inactivated parvovirus at six weeks of age.

An adorable Doberman puppy needs lots of care and attention, especially for the first few months of life. Make sure that you are able to devote yourself to raising your new pup properly.

When exposure isn't a factor, most veterinarians would rather wait to see the pup at eight weeks of age. At this point, they can also do a preliminary dental evaluation to see that all the puppy teeth are coming in correctly, check to see that the testicles are properly descending in males and make sure that there are no health reasons to prohibit vaccination at this time. Heart murmurs, wandering knee-caps (luxating patellae), juvenile cataracts, persistent hyperplastic primary vitreous (a congenital eye disease), and hernias are usually evident by this time.

Your veterinarian may also be able to perform temperament testing on the pup by eight weeks of age, or recommend someone to do it for you. Although temperament testing is not completely accurate, it can often predict which pups are the most anxious and fearful. Some form of temperament evaluation is important because behavioral problems account for more animals being euthanized (killed) each year than all medical conditions combined.

Recently, some veterinary hospitals have been recommending neutering pups as early as six to eight weeks of age. A study done at the University of Florida College of Veterinary Medicine over a span of more than four years concluded there was no increase in complications when animals were neutered at less than six months of age. The evaluators also concluded that the surgery appeared to be less stressful when done in young pups.

Most vaccination schedules consist of injections being given at 6-8, 10-12, and 14-16 weeks of age. Ideally, vaccines should not be given closer than two weeks apart, and three to four weeks apart seems to be optimal. Each vaccine usually consists of several different viruses (e.g., parvovirus, distemper, parainfluenza, hepatitis) combined into one injection. Coronavirus can be given as a separate vaccination according to the same schedule if pups are at risk. Some veterinarians and breeders advise another parvovirus booster at 18-20 weeks of age. A booster is given for all vaccines at one year of age, and annually thereafter. For animals at increased risk of exposure, parvovirus vaccination may be given as often as four times a year. A new vaccine for canine cough (tracheobronchitis) is squirted into the nostrils and can be given as early as six weeks of age if pups are at risk. Leptospirosis vaccination is given in some geographic areas and likely offers protection for six to eight months. The initial series consists of three to four injections spaced two to three weeks apart, starting as early as ten weeks of age. Rabies vaccine is given as a separate injection at three months of age, repeated when the pup is one year old, then repeated every one to three years depending on local risk and government regulation.

Some dogs have difficulty mounting a complete and protective response to vaccinations, especially Doberman Pinschers. In these cases, we typically recommend running a test to measure antibody titer (level) for parvovirus at 16 weeks of age and annually thereafter. This helps ensure that the vaccinations will, in fact, be protective.

A high-titer parvovirus vaccine, recently introduced in North America, is recommended for pups 6 to 18 weeks of age and does not interfere with the dam's protection. Nonetheless, certain lines of Rottweilers and Dobermans have been proven low or poor responders and may still be unable to mount a protective response.

Between 8 and 14 weeks of age, use every opportunity to expose the pup to as many people and situations as possible. This is part of the critical socialization period that will determine how

Breeders must socialize their Doberman puppies and acclimate them to human contact once they are a few weeks old. Breeders should not permit potential buyers to touch the pups until after the first set of inoculations at around six to eight weeks of age.

good a pet your dog will become. This is not the time to abandon a puppy for eight hours while you go to work. This is also not the time to punish your dog in any way, shape, or form.

This is the time to introduce your dog to neighborhood cats, birds, and other creatures. Hold off on exposure to other dogs until after the second vaccination in the series. You don't want your new friend to pick up contagious diseases from other dogs it meets before it has adequate protection. By 12 weeks of age, your pup should be ready for social outings with other dogs. Do it—it's a great way for your dog to feel comfortable around members of its own species. Walk the streets and introduce your pup to everybody you meet. Your goal should be to introduce your dog to every type of person or situation it is likely to encounter in life. Take it in cars, elevators, buses, subways, to parade grounds, parks, and beaches. You want your dog to habituate to all environments. Expose your pup to kids, teenagers, old people, people in wheelchairs, people on bicycles, people in uniforms. The more varied the exposure, the better the socialization.

Proper identification of your pet is also important since this minimizes the risk of theft and increases the chances that your pet will be returned to you if it is lost. There are several different options. Microchip implantation is a relatively painless procedure involving the subcutaneous injection of an implant the size of a grain of rice. This implant does not act as a beacon if your pet is missing. However, if your pet turns up at a veterinary clinic or shelter and is checked with a scanner, the chip provides information about you that can be used to quickly reunite you with your pet. This method of identifi-

cation is reasonably priced, permanent in nature, and performed at most veterinary clinics. Another option is tattooing, which can be done on the inner ear or on the skin of the abdomen. Most purebreds are given a number by the associated registry (e.g., American Kennel Club, United Kennel Club, Canadian Kennel Club, etc.) and this is used for identification, or permanent numbers such as social security numbers (telephone numbers and addresses may change during the life of your pet) can be used in the tattooing process. There are several different tattoo registries maintaining lists of dogs, their tattoo codes, and their owners. Finally, identification tags and collars provide quick information, but can be separated from your pet if it is lost or stolen. They work best when combined with a permanent identification system such as microchip implantation or tattooing.

FOUR TO SIX MONTHS OF AGE

At 16 weeks of age, when your pup gets the last in its series of regular induction vaccinations, ask your veterinarian about evaluating the pup for hip dysplasia with the PennHip™ technique. This helps predict the dog's risk of developing hip dysplasia as well as degenerative joint disease. Doberman breeders have done an excellent job decreasing the incidence of hip dysplasia through routine screening and registration programs. Since anesthesia is typically required for the procedure, many veterinarians like to do the evaluation at the same time as neutering.

At this time, it is very worthwhile to perform a diagnostic test for von Willebrand's disease, an inherited disorder that causes uncontrolled bleeding. This trait is very common in the Doberman Pinscher and some surveys report an incidence as high as 70%. A simple blood test is all that is required, but it may need to be sent to a special laboratory to have the test performed. You will be extremely happy that you had the foresight to have this done before neutering. If your dog does have a bleeding problem, it will be necessary to take special precautions during surgery. This is also a great time to run the parvovirus antibody titer to determine how well your dog has responded to the vaccination series.

SIX TO TWELVE MONTHS OF AGE

As a general rule, neuter your animal at about six months of age unless you fully intend to breed it. As we know, neutering can be safely done at eight weeks of age but this is still not a common practice. Neutering not only stops the possibility of pregnancy and inhibits undesirable behaviors but it can prevent several

It is important that Doberman puppies socialize with their littermates so that they are able to interact with other dogs later in life.

health problems as well. It is a well-established fact that female pups spayed before their first heat have a dramatically reduced incidence of mammary (breast) cancer. Likewise, neutered males significantly decrease their incidence of prostate disorders.

When your pet is six months of age, your veterinarian will want to take a blood sample to perform a heartworm test. If the test is negative and shows no evidence of heartworm infection, the pup will start heartworm prevention therapy. Some veterinarians are even recommending preventive therapy in younger pups. This might be a daily regimen, but newer therapies can be given on a once-a-month basis. As a bonus, most of these heartworm preventives also help prevent internal parasites.

If your Doberman has any patches of hair loss, your veterinarian will want to perform a skin scraping with a scalpel blade to see if any demodex mites are responsible. If there is a problem, don't lose hope; about 90% of demodicosis cases can be cured with supportive care only. However, it's important to diagnose it early before scarring results.

Another part of the six-month visit should be a thorough dental evaluation to make sure that all the permanent teeth have cor-rectly erupted. If they haven't, this will be the time to correct the problem. Correction should only be performed to make the animal more comfortable and promote normal chewing. The procedures should never be used to cosmetically improve the appearance of a dog used for show purposes or breeding.

After the dental evaluation, you should start implementing home dental care. In most cases, this will consist of brushing the teeth one or more times each week and perhaps using dental rinses. It is a sad fact that 85% of dogs over four years of age have periodontal disease and "doggy breath." In fact, it is so common that most people think it is normal. Well, it is normal—as normal as bad breath would be in people if they never brushed their teeth. Brush your dog's teeth regularly with a special toothbrush and toothpaste and you can greatly reduce the incidence of tartar buildup, bad breath, and gum disease. Provide the Puppy Bone™ from Nylabone® and a Gumabone® to puppies as early as eight to ten weeks. Nylabones® not only help in the proper development of the puppy's jaw and the emergence of adult teeth but help to keep the teeth clean...and the breath fresh. Better preventive care

Provide your puppy with a Gumabone® as early as eight to ten weeks of age. This Doberman pup is teething on a Plaque Attacker™, which is designed to maximize gum and teeth massage through its upraised "dental tips."

means that dogs live longer. They'll enjoy their sunset years more if they still have their teeth. Ask your veterinarian for details on home dental care.

THE FIRST SEVEN YEARS

At one year of age, your dog should be re-examined and have boosters for all vaccines. Your veterinarian will also want to do a very thorough physical examination to look for early evidence of problems. This might include taking radiographs (x-rays) of the hips and elbows to look for evidence of dysplastic changes. Genetic Disease Control (GDC) will certify hips and elbows at 12 months of age, but the Orthopedic Foundation for Animals (OFA) won't issue certification until 24 months of age.

At 12 months of age, it's also a great time to have some blood samples analyzed to provide background information. Although few Dobermans experience clinical problems at this young age, troubles may be starting. Therefore, it is a good idea to have baseline levels of thyroid hormones (free and total), TSH (thyroid-stimulating hormone), blood cell counts, organ chemistries, parvovirus antibody titers, and cholesterol levels. This can serve as a valuable comparison to samples collected in the fu-

ture. It may also help identify those Dobermans that develop liver disease (hepatitis) due to copper accumulation and poor immune response to vaccinations.

Each year, preferably around the time of your pet's birthday, it's time for another veterinary visit. This visit is a wonderful opportunity for a thorough clinical examination rather than just "shots." Since 85% of dogs have periodontal disease by four years of age, veterinary intervention does not seem to be as widespread as it should be. The examination should include visually inspecting the ears, eyes (a great time to start scrutinizing for progressive retinal atrophy, cataracts, etc.), mouth (don't wait for gum disease), and groin; listening (auscultation) to the lungs and heart; feeling (palpating) the lymph nodes and abdomen; and answering all of your questions about optimal health care. In addition, booster vaccinations are given, stool samples are checked for parasites, urine is analyzed, and blood samples may be collected for analysis. One of the tests run on the blood samples is for heartworm antigen. In areas of the country where heartworm is only present in the spring, summer, and fall (it's spread by mosquitoes), blood samples are collected and evaluated about a month prior to the mosquito season. Other routine blood tests are for blood cells (hematology), organ chemistries, thyroid levels, and electrolytes.

By two years of age, most veterinarians prefer to begin preventive dental cleanings, often referred to as "prophies." Anesthesia is required and the veterinarian or veterinary dentist will use an ultrasonic scaler to remove plaque and tartar from above and below the gum line and polish the teeth so that plaque has a harder time sticking to the teeth. Radiographs (x-rays) and fluoride treatments are other options. It is now known that it is plaque, not tartar, that initiates inflammation in the gums. Since scaling and root planing remove more tartar than plaque, veterinary dentists have begun using a new technique called PerioBUD (Periodontal Bactericidal Ultrasonic Debridement). The ultrasonic treatment is quicker, disrupts more bacteria and is less irritating to the gums. With tooth polishing to finish up the procedure, gum healing is better and owners can start home care sooner. Each dog has its own dental needs that must be addressed, but most veterinary dentists recommend prophies annually. Be sure that your Doberman always has a Nylabone® available to do his part in keeping his teeth clean.

At four to five years of age, your veterinarian will probably want to start screening for dilated cardiomyopathy, since this is more common in Doberman Pinschers than in all other breeds combined. Chest radiographs (x-rays) aren't usually too helpful; ultrasound examinations (echo-cardiography) and electrocardiograms (EKGs) are the preferred tests. Annual tests are usually sufficient and it is extremely important to diagnose the condition early because it is such a devastating and life-threatening disease.

SENIOR DOBERMANS

Doberman Pinschers are considered seniors when they reach about seven years of age. Veterinarians still usually only need to examine them once a year, but it is now important to start screening for geriatric problems. Accordingly, blood profiles, urinalysis, chest radiographs (x-rays), and electrocardiograms (EKGs) are recommended on an annual basis. When problems are caught early, they are much more likely to be successfully managed. This is as true in canine medicine as it is in human medicine.

MEDICAL PROBLEMS

RECOGNIZED GENETIC CONDITIONS SPECIFICALLY RELATED TO THE DOBERMAN PINSCHER

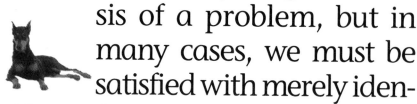

Many conditions appear to be especially prominent in Doberman Pinschers. Sometimes it is possible to identify the genetic basis of a problem, but in many cases, we must be satisfied with merely identifying the breeds that are at risk and how the conditions can be identified, treated, and prevented.

Facing page: Dilated cardiomyopathy is a serious condition that affects Doberman Pinschers. Routine veterinary examinations are very important, especially in young and middle-aged adults.

Following are some conditions that have been recognized as being common in the Doberman, but this listing is certainly not complete. Also, many genetic conditions may be common in certain breed lines, but not in the breed in general.

ACRAL LICK DERMATITIS (LICK GRANULOMA)

Few things are as frustrating to veterinarians as dealing with acral lick dermatitis, a problem caused by a dog licking incessantly at a spot on its leg. A dog will start licking at a spot and before you know it, it has removed layers of skin, leaving a raw open area. The reason for this is unknown, but many theories have come and gone and we're still not positive why a dog would do this kind of damage to itself.

Doberman Pinschers are, in most studies, the breed most commonly affected with this disorder and males are affected twice as often as females. Some recent research has shown that there may be some nerve deficits in dogs that develop this condition. Other research has suggested that boredom may be a precipitating cause that eventuates in a compulsive behavior.

It is important to diagnose these cases carefully since some cases may actually be a result of another disease condition, which will need to be addressed. Therefore, often biopsies, microbial cultures, and even radiographs (x-rays) are needed to help confirm a diagnosis.

Treatment is often frustrating because without knowing the cause it is difficult to predict the chances of success. Most therapies use anti-inflammatory agents but a variety of other options exist, including tranquilizers, female sex hormones, anti-anxiety drugs, and medications that reverse the effects of narcotics. More exotic treatments such as injecting cobra antivenin into the site, radiation therapy, and cryosurgery have been used in the past but have had limited success. The newest craze is to use anti-anxiety drugs and antidepressants to treat the "compulsive" aspect of the disorder.

Prevention is difficult because the ultimate cause of the problem has not yet been determined. Until we know more, our advice must be that affected dogs, their parents, and their siblings should not be used in breeding programs.

CATARACTS

Cataracts refer to an opacity or cloudiness on the lens and

ophthalmologists are careful to categorize them on the basis of stage, age of onset, and location. In Dobermans, cataracts can be inherited as a dominant trait (with variable expressivity) meaning that only one parent need carry the trait for pups to be affected. The cataracts are usually evident quite early, often in young pups, but almost always before one year of age. Many dogs adapt well to cataracts, but cataract removal surgery is available and quite successful if needed. The condition may be associated with persistent hyperplastic primary vitreous. Affected animals and their siblings should obviously not be used for breeding and careful ophthalmologic evaluation of both parents is warranted.

Any persistent cloudiness or opacity on the lens of your Doberman's eye should be checked out by a veterinarian.

CERVICAL VERTEBRAL INSTABILITY (WOBBLER SYNDROME)

Wobbler syndrome is caused by an instability in the intervertebral disks in the neck area and, once again, Doberman Pinschers are the main breed affected. When the disk destabilizes and puts pressure on the spinal cord, the result is severe neck pain. Unlike most other affected breeds, Dobermans may also develop rigid front legs. While affected Great Danes (another breed prone to the condition) start with problems between 3–18 months of age, Dobermans usually develop clinical signs later, between four and ten years of age. Affected dogs develop clinical signs (symptoms) associated with a narrowing of the spinal canal and compression of the spinal cord. Preliminary research suggests that excess dietary calcium, genetic factors, and overfeeding may all be involved.

The diagnosis is confirmed by taking radiographs (x-rays), and special dyes are often used

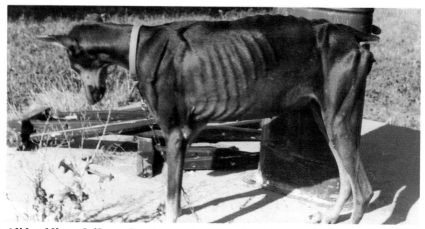

Ali had liver failure due to portosystemic shunt and died at less than one year of age. Her sire died of the same disease about eight months later. Owner, Robin Nuttall.

to help outline the defect. Strict rest and anti-inflammatory therapy (usually with corticosteroids) are used initially to quickly reduce the amount of inflammation in the spinal canal. This conservative therapy will often improve the clinical signs (symptoms) but cannot be expected to correct the underlying spinal defect. Some dogs can be maintained on long-term cortisone therapy with adequate control, but most others eventually develop progressive problems. If permanent damage is not evident, surgical decompression and stabilization is the treatment of choice.

The best way to prevent Wobbler syndrome in your Doberman is to avoid calcium supplementation, feed several small meals daily (rather than one large meal or ad libitum feedings), and not purchase a pup with a family history of vertebral instability. Unfortunately, since the condition isn't usually seen in this breed until relatively late in life, it is difficult or impossible for breeders to be aware of the condition when breeding young dogs. Several generations could actually be produced before anyone is aware of a problem.

COLOR DILUTION ALOPECIA

Color dilution alopecia, also known as color mutant alopecia, refers to the patchy poor haircoat that develops in animals bred for abnormally colored hair, especially those described as "blue" and "fawn."

The blues are diluted forms of the normal black and tan color, while fawns are diluted forms of red coloration. The colors may be interesting, but the hair follicles that produce them eventually become "dysplastic" and a variety of skin and fur problems result in virtually every blue and fawn Doberman. The coat is normal in pups, but eventually the abnormally colored hairs fall out and the skin becomes dry and scaly.

If there is any question about the cause of the problem, some of the abnormally colored hairs can be plucked and observed under a microscope or a skin biopsy can be taken and evaluated by a pathologist. There is no way to cure these dogs. Treatment is lifelong and includes the use of medicated shampoos and moisturizers. It is best not to own a "blue" or "fawn" and it is certainly a mistake to breed one unless you are a real enthusiast. These dogs require more care than the average owner is usually willing to provide.

Prevention is easy since there is no reason for the average pet owner to buy one of these color-diluted Dobermans—stick with blacks and reds. One day it should be possible for breeders to avoid Dobermans that carry the diluted gene, but for now,

prevention requires selecting breeding stock from animals that are normal in color and have never produced diluted pups. Dogs that have produced any diluted pups must be considered carriers for the trait.

DEMODICOSIS

Demodex mites are present on the skin of all dogs, but in some animals born with a defective immune system the numbers increase and begin to cause problems. Doberman Pinschers are usually cited as one of the breeds most commonly affected with this condition. Although it is thought to be genetically transmitted, the mode of transmission has never been conclusively demonstrated.

Most cases of demodicosis are seen in young pups and fully 90% of cases self-cure with little or no medical intervention by the time these dogs reach immunologic maturity at 18–36 months of age. In these cases, it is suspected that the immune system is marginally compromised and eventually matures and gets the condition under control. On the other hand, some pups (about 10% of those initially affected) do not get better and, in fact, become progressively worse. These are thought to have more severe immunologic compromise and are often labeled as having "generalized demodicosis."

The diagnosis is easily made by scraping the skin with a scalpel blade and looking at the collected debris under a microscope. The demodex mites are cigar-shaped and are easily seen. What is harder to identify is the immunologic defect that allowed the condition to occur in the first place. Recent research has suggested that the problem may be linked to a decrease in interleukin-2 response, but genetics is still a question.

If the cause of the immune dysfunction can be cured, the

To ensure the health of future generations of Doberman Pinschers, it is important to screen all potential breeding animals against congenital diseases.

mange will resolve on its own. Likewise, if the pup outgrows its immunologic immaturity or defect, the condition will self-cure. This process can best be assisted by ensuring that a healthy diet is being fed, treating for any internal parasites or other diseases, and perhaps using cleansing shampoos and nutritional supplements that help bolster the immune system. However, if the condition does not resolve on its own, or if it is getting worse despite conservative therapy, special mite-killing treatments are necessary. Amitraz (Mitaban®) is the most common dip used, but experimentally, milbemycin oxime (Interceptor®) and ivermectin (Ivomec®) given daily have shown some promising results. It must be remembered that killing the mites will not restore the immune system to normal.

Regarding prevention, it is best not to breed dogs with a history of demodicosis and dogs with generalized demodicosis should *never* be bred. Although the genetic nature of this disease has not been decisively proven, it doesn't make sense to add affected individuals to the gene pool of future generations.

DILATED CARDIOMYOPATHY

Dilated cardiomyopathy refers to a defect of the heart muscle in which the heart muscle becomes thin and stretched, much like a balloon. In that condition, it is not a very effective pump and, eventually, affected dogs die from heart failure. Doberman Pinschers are not only the most commonly affected breed, they are affected more than all other breeds combined. Thus, this is an extremely serious and deadly problem in the breed.

Although a genetic tendency is suspected, long-term studies are not yet available. In some breeds, a nutritional mechanism has been proposed and this might involve L-carnitine, taurine, and/or coenzyme Q. In Boxers, there appears to be an autosomal genetic association, likely dominant in nature. Recent studies in the American Cocker Spaniel seem to suggest that taurine (another amino acid) may be implicated, as it is in the feline form of the disease. However, it is impossible to extrapolate research from one breed to another. Until the research is done in Dobermans, we will just have to wait to draw conclusions. As if this isn't confusing enough, some researchers suspect that viruses might also be involved since there is some human research indicat-

ing that this might be the case in people.

Early in the course of the disease, affected animals seem normal. It is only when they show signs of heart failure that most owners seek veterinary attention. Early signs might include depression, coughing, exercise intolerance, weakness, respiratory distress, decreased appetite, and even fainting. In some breeds, and especially in the Doberman Pinscher, sudden death may be the first clue that something was ever wrong. Thus, routine thorough veterinary examinations are very important, especially in the young and middle-aged adult.

In some cases the heart rate is increased and this might indicate atrial fibrillation, a common sequel to cardiomyopathy. However, in most cases, radiographs (x-rays), electrocardiograms (EKGs), and echocardiograms (ultrasound examinations) are required for definitive diagnosis. In most breeds, x-rays reveal an enlarged heart, but the Doberman seems to be an exception in that heart size doesn't usually increase until late in the course of the disease. Echocardiograms are painless studies using ultrasound examination that are extremely useful in making the diagnosis. Electrocardiograms (EKGs) also have their place. Recent studies have shown that most dogs (especially Doberman Pinschers) with early cardiomyopathy have ventricular premature contractions (VPCs) which are indicators of increased risk to developing actual cardio-myopathy. These VPCs may not be evident all the time when EKGs are taken, so 24-hour studies with a Holter monitor are sometimes necessary, as they are in people.

There is no cure for cardiomyopathy, but some breeds respond well to megadoses of specific nutrients. However, there has been no specific

Fragmented coronoid process of the elbow, a manifestation of elbow dysplasia. Courtesy of Dr. Jack Henry.

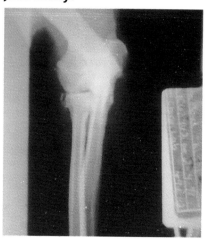

association with nutritional irregularities in the Doberman. Since these nutrients are quite safe, some individuals supplement with L-carnitine, taurine, and coenzyme Q even though they haven't been proven to be beneficial in the Doberman Pinscher. Digoxin (a digitalis derivative) is often used to treat the condition, as are beta-1 blockers and vasodilators. Milrinone, an experimental drug, has been very effective in dogs with heart muscle failure but is not yet available for dogs or people. All dogs with cardiomyopathy that are treated with drugs will only eventually succumb to the disease.

Right now there is no foolproof way to prevent cardiomyopathy. The best choice is to avoid pups that have a family history of cardiomyopathy. In many cases it will be necessary to know the medical history for at least the last three generations. A research project funded by the Doberman Pinscher Club of America is trying to determine the genetic link for cardiomyopathy using DNA testing. If that is successful, it may be possible to prevent the condition by selecting unaffected breeding partners based on tissue testing.

ELBOW DYSPLASIA

Elbow dysplasia doesn't refer to just one disease, but rather an entire range of disorders that affect the elbow joint. Several different processes might be involved, including ununited anconeal process, fragmented medial coronoid process, osteochondritis of the medial humeral condyle, or incomplete ossification of the humeral condyle. Elbow dysplasia and osteochondrosis are disorders of young dogs, with problems usually starting between four and seven months of age. The usual manifestation is a sudden onset of lameness. In time, the continued inflammation results in arthritis in the affected joints.

Dobermans that are allowed to exercise freely off-lead are at increased risk of elbow dysplasia, as they are more likely to sustain cartilage injuries.

Although Doberman Pinschers are often listed as being particularly prone to elbow dysplasia, the research says otherwise. Statistics compiled by the Orthopedic Foundation for Animals found that less than 3% of the Dobermans assessed up until December 31, 1994, have evidence of elbow dysplasia on radiographs (x-rays). However, since the incidence is so low, continued registration is recommended because it should be possible to completely eliminate the condition in Dobermans by conscientious breeding.

Radiographs (x-rays) are taken of the elbow joints and submitted to a registry for evaluation. The Orthopedic Foundation for Animals (OFA) will assign a breed registry number to those animals with normal elbows that are over 24 months of age. Abnormal elbows are reported as Grade I to III, where Grade III elbows have well-developed degenerative joint disease (arthritis). Normal elbows on individuals 24 months or older are assigned a breed registry number and are periodically reported to parent breed clubs. Genetic Disease Control (GDC) maintains an open registry for elbow dysplasia and assigns a registry number to those individuals with normal elbows at 12 months of age or older. Only animals with "normal" elbows should be used for breeding.

There is strong evidence to support the contention that osteochondrosis (OCD) of the elbow is an inherited disease, likely controlled by many genes. Preliminary research (in Labrador Retrievers) also suggests that the different forms of elbow dysplasia are inherited independently. Therefore, breeding stock should be selected from those animals without a history of osteochondrosis, preferably for several generations. Unaffected dogs producing offspring with OCD, FCP (fragmented coronoid process), or both, should not be bred again and unaffected first-degree relatives (e.g., siblings) should also not be used for breeding.

The most likely associations made to date suggest that, other than genetics, feeding diets high in calories, calcium, and protein promotes the development of osteochondrosis in susceptible dogs. Also, animals that are allowed to exercise in an unregulated fashion are at increased risk, since they are more likely to sustain cartilage injuries.

The management of dogs with OCD is a matter of much debate and controversy. Some recommend surgery to remove the damaged cartilage before permanent damage is done. Others recommend conservative therapy of rest and pain-killers. The most common drugs used are aspirin and polysulfated glycosaminoglycans. Most veterinarians agree that the use of cortisone-like compounds (corticosteroids) creates more problems than it treats in this condition. What seems clear is that some dogs will respond to conservative therapies, while others will need surgery. Surgery is often helpful if performed before there is significant joint damage.

FLANK SUCKING

Flank sucking is a poorly understood condition in which dogs (almost exclusively Doberman Pinschers) nurse (suck) patches of skin on their flanks. Many theories have been proposed for the cause of this disorder but none have been confirmed. The current thought is that it might represent a form of psychomotor epilepsy or a compulsive (stereotypic) behavior. Whatever the cause, this condition can be troubling for owner and dog, but rarely is it associated with actual illness.

Treatment is usually disappointing (since the actual cause is rarely treated) but the quality of life is not usually affected in these dogs. Some respond to an Elizabethan collar worn around the neck which denies access to the area. In most cases the response is temporary and recurrence is common once the collar is removed. Bitter-tasting substances may be applied to the area and this is sometimes effective. In other cases, the animals will eventually nurse the area despite the application of these products. Behavior modification using techniques such as counterconditioning is also effective in some cases, but constant monitoring is required to get consistent results. Finally, drugs used to treat compulsive disorders (e.g., fluoxetine, clomipramine) or epilepsy (e.g., primidone) can sometimes yield very satisfactory results but should be considered as a final option because they often require lifelong administration. Although the exact cause of flank sucking is still not known, affected animals should not be used for breeding. At this time there is at least presumptive evidence that the condition runs in families.

GASTRIC DILATATION/ VOLVULUS (BLOAT)

Gastric dilatation (bloat) occurs when the stomach becomes distended with air. The air gets swallowed into the stomach when susceptible dogs exercise, gulp their food/water, or are stressed. Although bloat can occur at any age, it becomes more common as susceptible dogs get older. Purebreds are three times more likely to suffer from bloat than mutts. Doberman Pinschers are susceptible to the condition and frequently appear in lists of "breeds most prone to bloat." Recent surveys have found that Doberman Pinschers are not as prone as other deep-chested breeds such as Great Danes, Weimaraners, Saint Bernards, Gordon Setters, Irish Setters, Boxers, and Standard Poodles.

Bloat on its own is uncomfortable, but the possible consequences make it life-threatening. As the stomach fills with air like a balloon, it can twist on itself and impede the flow of food within the stomach as well as the blood supply to the stomach and other digestive organs. This twisting (volvulus or torsion) not only makes the bloat worse, but also results in toxins being released into the bloodstream and death of blood-de-

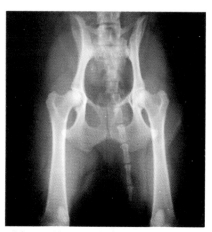

This radiograph displays a dog that received an OFA "excellent" when x-rayed for hip dysplasia. Both of the hip joints are clear of dysplasia.

prived tissues. These events, if allowed to progress, will usually result in death in four to six hours. Approximately one-third of dogs with bloat and volvulus will die, even under appropriate hospital care.

Affected dogs will be uncomfortable, restless, depressed, and have extended abdomens. They need veterinary attention immediately or they will suffer from shock and die! There are a variety of surgical procedures to correct the abnormal positioning of the stomach and organs. Intensive medical therapy is also necessary to treat for shock, acidosis, and the effects of toxins.

Bloat can't be completely pre-vented, but there are some easy things to do to greatly reduce risk. Don't leave food down for dogs to eat as they wish. Divide the day's meals into three portions and feed in the morning, afternoon, and evening. Try not to let your dog gulp its food; if necessary, add some chew toys to the bowl so he has to work around them to get the food. Add water to dry food before feeding. Have fresh, clean water available all day but not at mealtime. Do not allow exercise for one hour before and after meals. Following this feeding advice may actually save your dog's life. Contrary to popular belief, there have been no studies that support the contention that soy in the diet increases the risk of bloat. Soy is relatively poorly digested and can lead to flatulence, but the gas accumulation in bloat comes from swallowed air, not from gas produced in the intestines.

HIP DYSPLASIA

Hip dysplasia is a genetically transmitted developmental problem of the hip joint that is common in many breeds. Dogs may be born with a "susceptibility" or "tendency" to develop hip dysplasia, but it is not a foregone conclusion that all susceptible dogs will eventually develop hip dysplasia. All dysplastic dogs are born with normal hips and the dysplastic changes begin within the first 24 months of life, although they are usually evident long before then.

It is now known that there are several factors that help determine whether a susceptible dog will ever develop hip dysplasia. These include body size, conformation, growth patterns, caloric load, and electrolyte balance in the dog food.

Although Doberman Pinschers are often cited as being prone to hip dysplasia, research tabulated up to January, 1995, by the Orthopedic Foundation for Animals concluded that less than 7% of the radiographs submitted from Doberman Pinschers had evidence of hip dysplasia. This is great news because the Doberman breeders have been able to reduce the incidence in the breed by over 60% just through conscientious breeding.

When purchasing a Doberman pup, it is best to ensure that the parents were both registered with normal hips through one of the international registries such as the Orthopedic Foundation for Animals or Genetic Disease Control. Pups over 16 weeks of age can be tested by veterinarians trained

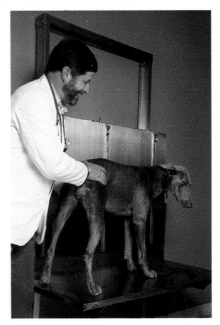

Veterinarians can provide screening services for hip dysplasia as well as regular checkups and inoculations. The test for hip dysplasia requires an x-ray under anesthesia (most commonly).

in the PennHip™ procedure, which is a way of predicting a dog's risk of developing hip dysplasia and arthritis. In time, it should be possible to completely eradicate hip dysplasia from the breed.

If you start with a pup with less risk of hip dysplasia, you can further reduce your risk by controlling its environment. Select a food with a moderate amount of protein and avoid the super-premium and high-calorie diets. Also, feed your pup several times a day for defined periods (e.g., 15 minutes) rather than leaving the food down all day. Avoid all nutritional supplements, especially those that include calcium, phosphorus, and/or vitamin D. Use controlled exercise for your pup rather than letting him run loose. Unrestricted exercise can stress the pup's joints, which are still developing.

If you have a dog with hip dysplasia, all is not lost. There is much variability in the clinical presentation. Some dogs with severe dysplasia experience little pain, while others that have only minor changes may be extremely sore. The main problem is that dysplastic hips promote degenerative joint disease (osteoarthritis or osteoarthrosis) which can eventually incapacitate the joint. Aspirin and other anti-inflammatory agents are suitable in the early stages; surgery is needed when animals are in great pain, when drug therapy doesn't work adequately, or when movement is severely compromised.

HYPOTHYROIDISM

Hypothyroidism is the most commonly diagnosed endocrine (hormonal) problem in the Doberman Pinscher. The disease itself refers to an insufficient amount of thyroid hormones being produced. Although there are several different potential causes, lymphocytic thyroiditis is by far the most common. Iodine deficiency and goiter are extremely rare. In lymphocytic thyroiditis, the body produces antibodies that target aspects of thyroid tissue. The process usually starts between one and three years of age in affected animals, but doesn't become clinically evident until later in life.

There is a great deal of misinformation about hypothyroidism. Owners often expect that affected dogs will be obese with the condition, and otherwise don't suspect a problem. The fact is that hypothyroidism is quite variable in its manifestations and obesity is only seen in a small percentage of cases. In most cases, affected animals appear fine until they use up most of their remaining thyroid hormone reserves. The most common manifestations, then, are lack of energy and recurrent infections. Hair loss is seen in about one-third of the cases.

You might suspect that hypothyroidism would be easy to diagnose, but it is trickier than you may think. Since there is a large reserve of thyroid hormones in the body, a test measuring only total blood levels of the hormones (T-4 and T-3) is not a very sensitive indicator of the condition. Thyroid stimulation tests are the best way to measure the functional reserve. Measuring "free" and "total" levels of the hormones and endogenous TSH (thyroid-stimulating hormone) are other approaches. Also, since we know that most cases are due to antibodies produced in the body, screening for these autoantibodies can help identify animals at risk of developing hypothyroidism.

Because this breed is so prone to developing hypothyroidism, periodic "screening" for the disorder is warranted in many cases. Although none of the screening tests are perfect, a basic panel evaluating total T-4, free T-4, TSH, and cholesterol levels is a good start. Ideally, this would first be performed at one year of age and annually thereafter. This "screening" is practical, because none of these tests is very expensive.

Fortunately, although there may be some problems in diagnosing hypothyroidism, treatment is straightforward and relatively inexpensive. Supple-menting the affected animal twice daily with thyroid hormone effectively treats the condition. In many breeds, supplementation with thyroid hormones is commonly done to help confirm the diagnosis. However, since thyroid hormones affect the heart, and since Doberman Pinschers are so prone to the heart disease cardiomyopathy, thyroid hormone supplementation should be reserved for those animals with well-documented hypothyroidism. Animals with hypothyroidism should not be used in a breeding program and those with circulating autoantibodies but no actual hypothyroid disease should also not be used for breeding.

LIVER DISEASE DUE TO COPPER ACCUMULATION

Some dogs are prone to developing liver disease in association with an inherited metabolic defect which causes copper to accumulate in the liver and can lead to toxicity. This is similar to Wilson's disease in people. The Doberman Pinscher is not the breed affected most often (that would be the Bedlington Terrier), but the incidence is high enough to warrant mention here. The condition is spread as a recessive trait so both parents must be carriers if a dog is found to be affected.

Affected dogs develop a slowly progressive form of liver disease. They are usually in young adulthood when the condition is first recognized. Jaundice only develops late in the course of the disease when liver function is severely compromised.

Very recently, researchers have discovered a genetic marker for copper toxicosis that can be detected by a blood test. Although not yet widely available as a commercial test, this laboratory evaluation is an exceptionally important method for detecting carriers of the dis-

ease. Carriers should be removed from all breeding programs, making it possible to eventually completely eliminate the trait in Doberman Pinschers.

NARCOLEPSY

Narcolepsy is a sleep disorder in which animals may spontaneously fall asleep without association to tiredness. It has been documented in at least 15 breeds of dogs but the inheritance has been studied in only three—the Doberman Pinscher, Labrador Retriever, and Miniature Poodle. In the Doberman, the condition is passed along as a simple autosomal recessive trait. Thus, both parents must be carriers (yet normal) to pass

You can't confuse a pooped-out puppy with a sleeping disorder. Narcolepsy is marked by spontaneous episodes of falling asleep. Dobermans have proven more prone to the disorder than most other breeds, though it is not common in any breed.

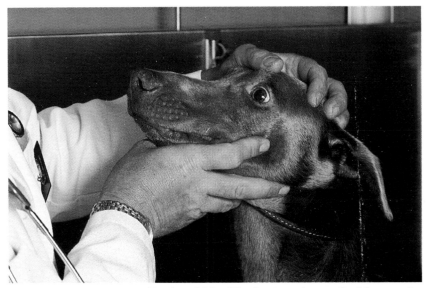

Your Doberman's pupils should be black. Any signs of white on the pupil, known as leukocoria, could be an indication of persistent hyperplastic primary vitreous, which is a congenital eye disease most commonly reported in the Doberman Pinscher.

the trait to the pups. Affected pups usually start to have problems between 4 and 20 weeks of age; they often have more attacks as they get excited or try to eat or sleep. The condition can be conclusively diagnosed based on food-elicited cataplexy testing, should that prove necessary. Various drugs such as yohimbine and imipramine have been used in treatment but many Dobermans tend to have fewer attacks as they get older.

The condition can be prevented if relatives of affected pups are not used in breeding.

This includes normal siblings, parents and their siblings, and grandparents and their siblings. Hopefully we'll have a predictive test one day so that potential breeding pairs can be screened, but that is not an option at present.

PERSISTENT HYPERPLASTIC PRIMARY VITREOUS

Persistent hyperplastic primary vitreous (PHPV) is a congenital eye disease which is most commonly reported in the Doberman Pinscher. It results from a failure of the hyaloid artery in the eye to regress; the result is a scarring process (fibroplasia). Clinically, this can cause a white pupil (leukocoria) as the scar tissue adheres to the back of the lens. There are a number of other problems that can be associated with the condition, including cataracts, persistent pupillary membranes, retinal dysplasia, lens coloboma, and luxation of the lens. Research has shown it to be an inherited trait in the Doberman Pinscher and a multiple locus inheritance pattern has been suggested. Affected animals can often be successfully treated, but recovered Dobermans and their close relatives should not be bred for fear of propagating the condition further.

Research and development of drug therapies in canine medicine are advancing at a rapid pace. Ask your veterinarian about new vaccinations.

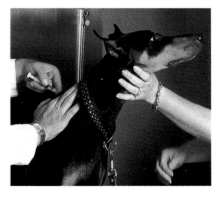

SULFA SENSITIVITY

Sulfas are drugs used to treat bacterial infections. They are also used, in some cases, for treating chronic colitis and some other immunologic problems. Although sulfa drugs are generally considered extremely safe, some Doberman Pinschers appear to be extremely sensitive to these products and fatalities have been reported. In other reports, arthritis involving multiple joints (nonseptic polyarthritis) and hepatitis have been reported. This extreme reaction seems to be peculiar to Dobermans, suggesting a definite breed sensitivity. Since there are many different antibiotics available, it is best to avoid the use of sulfa drugs in all Doberman Pinschers until the condition is better understood.

VON WILLEBRAND'S DISEASE

Von Willebrand's disease (vWD) is the most commonly inherited bleeding disorder of dogs. The abnormal gene can be inherited from one or both parents. If both parents pass on the gene, most of the resultant pups fail to thrive and most will die. In most cases, though, the pup inherits a relative lack of clotting ability which is quite variable. For instance, one dog may have 15% of the clotting factor, while another might have 60%. The higher the amount, the less likely it will be that the bleeding will be readily evident since spontaneous bleeding is usually only seen when dogs have less than 30% of the normal level of von Willebrand clotting factor. Thus, some dogs don't get diagnosed until they are neutered or spayed and they end up bleeding uncontrollably or they develop pockets of blood (hematomas) at the surgical site. In addition to the inherited form of vWD, this disorder can also be acquired in association with familial hypothyroidism. This form is usually seen in Doberman Pinschers older than five years of age.

Von Willebrand's disease is extremely important in the Doberman Pinscher because the incidence appears to be on the rise. In at least one study, up to 70% of the Dobermans for which samples were submitted had evidence of the disease. However, there is good news. There are tests available to determine the amount of von Willebrand factor in the blood, and they are accurate and reasonably priced. Dobermans used for breeding should have normal amounts of von Willebrand factor in their

blood and so should all pups that are adopted as household pets. Carriers should not be used for breeding, even if they appear clinically normal. Since hypothyroidism can be linked with von Willebrand's disease, thyroid profiles can also be a useful part of the screening procedure in older Dobermans.

OTHER CONDITIONS SEEN IN THE DOBERMAN

- Acne
- Anterior Chamber Cleavage Syndrome
- Atherosclerosis
- Bullous Pemphigoid
- Bundle of His Degeneration
- Congenital Vestibular Disease
- Craniomandibular Osteopathy
- Cutaneous Tag
- Defective Neutrophil Function
- Diabetes Mellitus
- Deafness
- Enophthalmos
- Epilepsy
- Eversion of Third Eyelid Cartilage
- Histiocytoma
- Ichthyosis
- Intervertebral Disk Disease
- Nevus (Adnexal)
- Oligodontia (Missing Premolars)
- Osteosarcoma
- Pemphigus Foliaceus
- Persistent Hyperplastic Tunica Vasculosa Lentis
- Persistent Pupillary Membranes
- Persistent Right Aortic Arch
- Polydontia
- Polyostotic Fibrous Dysplasia
- Portosystemic Shunt
- Primary Ciliary Dyskinesia
- Progressive Retinal Atrophy
- Renal Hypoplasia/Dysplasia
- Retinal Dysplasia (Retinal Folds)
- Sleep Disorders
- Systemic Lupus Erythematosus
- Vitiligo
- Wry Mouth

INFECTIONS & INFESTATIONS

**HOW TO PROTECT YOUR DOBERMAN PINSCHER
FROM PARASITES AND MICROBES**

An important part of keeping your Doberman Pinscher healthy is to prevent problems caused by parasites and microbes. Although there are a variety of drugs available that can help limit problems, prevention is always the desired option. Taking the proper precautions leads to less aggravation, less itching, and less expense.

Facing page: This Doberman puppy has demodectic mange; it is only visible on her paws at this point but it will eventually spread to her head and body.

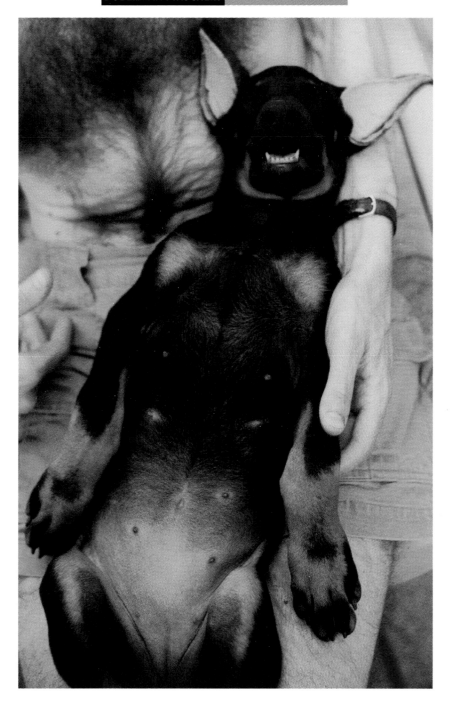

FLEAS

Fleas are common parasites but not an inevitable part of every pet owner's reality. If you take the time to understand some of the basics of flea population dynamics, control is both conceivable and practical.

Fleas have four life stages (egg, larva, pupa, adult) and each stage responds to some therapies while being resistant to others. Failing to understand this is the major reason why some people have so much trouble getting the upper hand in the battle to control fleas.

Fleas spend all their time on dogs and only leave if physically removed by brushing, bathing, or scratching. However, the eggs that are laid on the animal are not sticky and fall to the ground, contaminating the environment. Our goal must be to remove fleas from the animals in the house, from the house itself, and from the immediate outdoor environment. Part of our plan must also involve using different medications to get rid of the different life stages as well as minimizing the use of potentially harmful insecticides that could be poi-

Fleas have four life stages: egg, larva, pupa, adult. Photo courtesy of Fleabusters, Rx for Fleas, Inc.

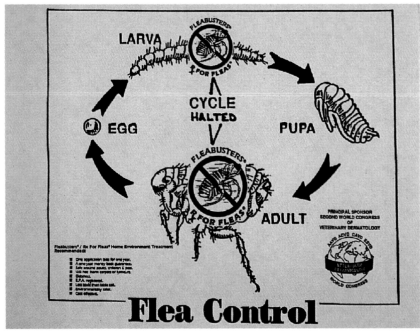

Flea Control

sonous to pets and family members.

A flea comb is a very handy device for recovering fleas from pets. The best places to comb are the tailhead, groin area, armpits, back, and neck region. Collected fleas should be dropped into a container of alcohol, which will quickly kill them before they can escape. In addition, all pets should be bathed with a cleansing shampoo or flea shampoo to remove fleas and eggs. This has no residual effect, however, and fleas can jump back on immediately after the bath if nothing else is done. Rather than using potent insecticidal dips and sprays, consider products containing safe pyrethrins, imidacloprid or fipronil and insect growth regulators (such as methoprene and pyripoxyfen) or insect development inhibitors (IDIs) such as lufenuron. These products are not only extremely safe, but the combination is effective against eggs, larvae, and adults. This only leaves the pupal stage to cause continued problems. Insect growth regulators can also be safely given as once-a-month oral preparations. Electronic flea collars are not to be recommended for any dogs.

To clean up the household, vacuuming is a good first step because it picks up about 50% of

Before you let your Doberman outside, especially in the warmer months, he should be protected against flea infestation. Consider products containing safe pyrethrins and insect growth regulators.

the flea eggs and it also stimulates flea pupae to emerge as adults, a stage when they are easier to kill with insecticides. The vacuum bag should be removed and discarded with each treatment. Household treatment can then be initiated with pyrethrins and a combination of either insect growth regulators or sodium polyborate (a borax derivative). The pyrethrins need to be reapplied every two to three weeks but the insect growth regulators last about two to three months and many companies guarantee sodium polyborate for a full year. Stronger insecticides such as carbamates and organophosphates can be used and will last three to four weeks in the household, but they are potentially toxic and offer no real advantages other than their persistence in the home environment. This is also one of their major disadvantages.

When an insecticide is combined with an insect growth regulator, flea control is most likely to be successful. The insecticide kills the adult fleas and the insect growth regulator affects the eggs and larvae. However, insecticides kill less than 20% of flea cocoons (pupae). Because of this, new fleas may hatch in two to three weeks despite appropriate application of products. This is known as the "pupal window" and is one of the most common obstacles to effective flea control. This is why a safe insecticide should be applied to the home environment two to three weeks after the initial treatment. This catches the newly hatched pupae before they have

a chance to lay eggs and perpetuate the flea problem.

If treatment of the outdoor environment is needed, there are several options. Pyripoxyfen an insect growth regulator, is stable in sunlight and can be used outdoors. Sodium polyborate can be used as well, but it is important that it not be inadvertently eaten by pets. Organophosphates and carbamates are sometimes recommended for outdoor use. It is not necessary to treat the entire property—flea control should be directed predominantly at garden margins, porches, dog houses, garages, and other pet lounging areas. Fleas don't do well in direct exposure to sunlight, so generalized lawn treatment is not needed. Finally, microscopic worms (nematodes) are available that can be sprayed onto the lawn with a garden sprayer. The nematodes eat immature flea forms and then biodegrade without harming anything else.

TICKS

Ticks are found world-wide and can cause a variety of problems including blood loss, tick paralysis, Lyme disease, "tick fever," Rocky Mountain Spotted Fever, and babesiosis. All are important diseases which need to be prevented whenever possible. This is only possible by limiting our pets' exposure to ticks.

For those species of tick that dwell indoors, the eggs are laid mostly in cracks and on vertical surfaces in kennels and homes. Most other species are found outside in vegetation, such as grassy meadows, woods, brush, and weeds.

Ticks feed only on blood but they don't actually bite. They attach to a host by sticking their harpoon-shaped mouthparts into the host's skin and sucking blood. Some ticks can increase their size 20–50 times as they feed. They are often found between the toes and in the ears, although they can appear anywhere on the host's skin surface.

A good approach to preventing ticks is to remove underbrush and leaf litter, and to thin the trees in areas where dogs are allowed. This removes the cover and food sources for small mammals that serve as hosts for ticks. Ticks must have adequate cover that provides high levels of moisture and at the same time provides an opportunity for contact with animals. Keeping the lawn well maintained also makes ticks less likely to drop by and stay.

Because of the potential for ticks to transmit a variety of harmful diseases, dogs should be carefully inspected after walks

A good approach to preventing ticks is to remove underbrush and leaf litter from your lawn. Keeping your lawn well-maintained makes it less likely for ticks to drop by and stay.

through wooded areas (where ticks may be found) and any ticks should be removed carefully and promptly. Care should be taken not to squeeze, crush, or puncture the tick's body since exposure to the tick's body fluids may lead to the spread of any disease carried by that tick to the animal or to the person removing the tick. The tick should be disposed of in a container of alcohol or flushed down the toilet. If the site becomes infected, veterinary attention should be sought immediately. Insecticides and repellents should only be applied to pets following appropriate veterinary advice, since indiscriminate use can be dangerous. Recently, a new tick collar has become available which contains amitraz. This collar not only kills ticks but causes them to retract from the skin within two to three days. This greatly reduces the chances of ticks transmitting a variety of diseases. A spray formulation has also recently been developed and marketed. It might seem that there should be vaccines for all the diseases carried by ticks, but only a Lyme disease *(Borrelia burgdorferi)* vaccine is currently available.

MANGE

Mange refers to any skin condition caused by mites. The contagious mites include ear mites, scabies mites, cheyletiella mites, and chiggers. Demodectic mange is associated with proliferation of demodex mites, but they are not considered contagious.

The most common causes of mange in dogs are ear mites, and these are extremely contagious. The best way to avoid ear mites is to buy pups from sources that don't have problems with ear mite infestation. Otherwise, pups readily acquire them when kept in crowded environments in which other animals might be carriers. Treatment is effective if

whole body (or systemic) therapy is used, but relapses are common when medication in the ear canal is the only approach. This is because the mites tend to crawl out of the ear canal when medications are applied. They simply feed elsewhere on the body until it is safe for them to return to the ears.

Scabies mites and cheyletiella mites are passed on by other dogs that are carrying the mites. They are "social" diseases that can be prevented by avoiding exposure of your dog to others that are infested. Scabies (sarcoptic mange) has the dubious honor of being the most itchy disease to which dogs are susceptible. Chigger mites are present in forested areas and dogs acquire them by roaming in these areas. All types of mites can be effectively diagnosed and treated by your veterinarian should your dog happen to become infested.

HEARTWORM

Heartworm disease is caused by the worm *Dirofilaria immitis* and is spread by mosquitoes. The female heartworms produce microfilariae (baby worms) that circulate in the bloodstream, waiting to be picked up by mosquitoes to pass the infection along. Dogs do not get heartworm by socializing with infected dogs; they only get infected by mosquitoes that carry the infective microfilariae. The adult heartworms grow in the heart and major blood vessels and eventually cause heart failure.

Fortunately, heartworm is easily prevented by safe oral medications that can be administered daily or on a once-a-month basis. The once-a-month preparations also help prevent many of the common intestinal parasites, such as hookworms, roundworms, and whipworms.

Prior to giving any preventive medication for heartworm, an antigen test (an immunologic test that detects heartworms) should be performed by a veterinarian since it is dangerous to give the medication to dogs that harbor the parasite. Some experts also recommend a microfilarial test, just to be doubly certain. Once the test results show that the dog is free of heartworms, the preventive therapy can be commenced. The length of time the heartworm preventives must be given depends on the length of the mosquito season. In some parts of the country, dogs are on preventive therapy year round. Heartworm vaccines may soon be available but the preventives now available are easy to administer and quite safe.

INTESTINAL PARASITES

The most important internal parasites in dogs are roundworms, hookworms, tapeworms, and whipworms. Roundworms are the most common. It has been estimated that 13 trillion roundworm eggs are discharged in dog feces every day! Studies have shown that 75% of all pups carry roundworms and start shedding them by three weeks of age. People are infected by exposure to dog feces containing infective roundworm eggs, not by handling pups. Hookworms can cause a disorder known as cutaneous larva migrans in people. In dogs, they are most dangerous to puppies since they latch onto the intestines and suck blood. They can cause anemia and even death when they are present in large numbers. The most common tapeworm is *Dipylidium caninum* which is spread by fleas. However, another tapeworm (*Echinococcus multilocularis*) can cause fatal disease in people and can be spread to people from dogs. Whipworms live in the lower aspects of the intestines. Dogs get whipworms by consuming infective larvae. However, it may be another three months before they start shedding them in their stool, greatly complicating diagnosis. In other words, a dog can be infected by whipworms, but fecal evaluations are usually negative until the dog starts passing the eggs three months after becoming infected.

Other parasites, such as coccidia, cryptosporidium, giardia, and flukes can also cause problems in dogs. The best way to prevent all internal parasite problems is to have pups dewormed according to your veterinarian's recommendations, and to have parasite checks done on a regular basis, at least annually.

VIRAL INFECTIONS

Dogs get viral infections such as distemper, hepatitis, parvovirus, and rabies by exposure to infected animals. The key to prevention is controlled exposure to other animals and, of course, vaccination. Today's vaccines are extremely effective and properly vaccinated dogs are at minimal risk for contracting these diseases. However, it is still important to limit exposure to other animals that might be harboring infection. This is particularly important for Doberman Pinschers because this breed tends to form the weakest protection following vaccination. In fact, we recommend performing tests on parvovirus antibody levels in vaccinated Dobermans to make sure they have produced adequate amounts of antibody. Thus, limiting exposure to carriers is particularly important in this breed. When selecting a facility for boarding or grooming, make sure the facility limits its clientele to animals that have documented vaccine histories. This is in everyone's best interest. Similarly, make sure your veterinarian has a quarantine area for infected dogs and that animals aren't admitted for surgery, boarding, grooming, or diagnostic testing without up-to-date vaccinations. By controlling exposure and ensuring vaccination, your pet should be safe from these potentially devastating diseases.

It is beyond the scope of this book to settle all the controversies of vaccination but they are worth mentioning. Should vaccines be combined in a single injection? It's convenient and cheaper to do it this way, but might some vaccine ingredients interfere with others? Some say yes, some say no. Are vaccine schedules designed for convenience or effectiveness? Mostly convenience. Some ingredients may only need to be given every two or more years, but research is incomplete. Should the dose of the vaccine vary with weight or should a Chihuahua receive the same dose as a Doberman Pinscher? Given their vaccination response, should Doberman Pinschers receive higher vaccine dosages than other dogs? Good questions, no definitive answers. Finally, should we be using modified-live or inactivated vaccine products? There is no short answer for this debate. Ask your veterinarian and do a lot of reading yourself!

CANINE COUGH

Canine infectious tracheobronchitis, also known as canine cough and kennel cough, is a contagious viral/bacterial disease that results in a hacking cough that may persist for many weeks. It is common wherever dogs are kept in close quarters, such as kennels, grooming parlors, dog shows, training classes, and even veterinary clinics. The condition doesn't respond well to most medications, but eventually clears spontaneously over the course of many weeks. Pneumonia is a possible but uncommon complication.

Prevention is best achieved by limiting exposure and having your dog vaccinated. The fewer opportunities you give your dog to come in contact with others, the less the likelihood of getting infected. Vaccination is not fool-

Make sure your Doberman puppy is properly vaccinated before he comes in contact with other dogs. Up until six to eight weeks of age, puppies receive maternal antibodies through nursing and should only be exposed to their dam and littermates at this time.

proof because many different viruses can be involved. Parainfluenza virus is included in most vaccines and is one of the more common viruses known to initiate the condition. *Bordetella bronchiseptica* is the bacterium most often associated with tracheobronchitis and a vaccine is now available that needs to be repeated twice yearly for dogs at risk. This vaccine is squirted into the nostrils to help stop the infection before it gets deeper into the respiratory tract. Make sure the vaccination is given several days (preferably two weeks) before exposure to ensure maximum protection.

FIRST AID

by Judy Iby, RVT

KNOWING YOUR DOG IN GOOD HEALTH

With some experience, you will learn how to give your dog a physical at home, and consequently will learn to recognize many potential problems. If you can detect a problem early, you can seek timely medical help and thereby decrease your dog's risk of developing a more serious problem.

Facing page: Chewing on sticks can be very dangerous for your Doberman Pinscher puppy. A piece could break off and he could choke on it.

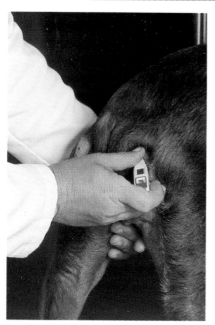

It is easiest to take your Doberman's temperature with the dog in a standing position. Make sure to hold on to the thermometer so that it isn't expelled or sucked in.

Every pet owner should be able to take his pet's temperature, pulse, respirations, and check the capillary refill time (CRT). Knowing what is normal will alert the pet owner to what is abnormal, and this can be life saving for the sick pet.

TEMPERATURE
The dog's normal temperature is 100.5 to 102.5 degrees Fahrenheit. Take the temperature rectally for at least one minute. Be sure to shake the thermometer down first, and you may find it helpful to lubricate the end. It is easy to take the temperature with the dog in a standing position. Be sure to hold on to the thermometer so that it isn't expelled or sucked in. A dog could have an elevated temperature if he is excited or if he is overheated; however, a high temperature could indicate a medical emergency. On the other hand, if the temperature is below 100 degrees, this could also indicate an emergency.

CAPILLARY REFILL TIME AND GUM COLOR
It is important to know how your dog's gums look when he is healthy, so you will be able to recognize a difference if he is not feeling well. There are a few breeds, among them the Chow Chow and its relatives, that have black gums and a black tongue. This is normal for them. In general, a healthy dog will have bright pink gums. Pale gums are an indication of shock or anemia and are an emergency. Likewise, any yellowish tint is an indication of a sick dog. To check capillary refill time (CRT) press your thumb against the dog's gum. The gum will blanch out (turn white) but should refill (return to the normal pink color) in

one to two seconds. CRT is very important. If the refill time is slow and your dog is acting poorly, you should call your veterinarian immediately.

HEART RATE, PULSE, AND RESPIRATIONS

Heart rate depends on the breed of the dog and his health. Normal heart rates range from about 50 beats per minute in the larger breeds to 130 beats per minute in the smaller breeds. You can take the heart rate by pressing your fingertips on the dog's chest. Count for either 10 or 15 seconds, and then multiply by either 6 or 4 to obtain the rate per minute. A normal pulse is the same as the heart rate and is taken at the femoral artery located on the insides of both rear legs. Respirations should be observed and depending on the size and breed of the dog should be 10 to 30 per minute. Obviously, illness or excitement could account for abnormal rates.

PREPARING FOR AN EMERGENCY

It is a good idea to prepare for an emergency by making a list and keeping it by the phone. This list should include:

1. Your veterinarian's name, address, phone number, and office hours.

2. Your veterinarian's policy for after-hour care. Does he take his own emergencies or does he refer them to an emergency clinic?

3. The name, address, phone number and hours of the emergency clinic your veterinarian uses.

4. The number of the National Poison Control Center for Animals in Illinois: 1-800-548-2423. It is open 24 hours a day.

In a true emergency, time is of the essence. Some signs of an

At eight and a half years of age, Jasmine only has three legs—but that doesn't slow her down one bit.

emergency may be:

1. Pale gums or an abnormal heart rate.
2. Abnormal temperature, lower than 100 degrees or over 104 degrees.
3. Shock or lethargy.
4. Spinal paralysis.

A dog hit by car needs to be checked out and probably should have radiographs of the chest and abdomen to rule out pneumothorax or ruptured bladder.

EMERGENCY MUZZLE

An injured, frightened dog may not even recognize his owner and may be inclined to bite. If your dog should be in-jured, you may need to muzzle him to protect yourself before you try to handle him. It is a good idea to practice muzzling the calm, healthy dog so you understand the technique. Slip a lead over his head for control. You can tie his mouth shut with something like a two-foot-long bandage or piece of cloth. A necktie, stocking, leash or even a piece of rope will also work.

1. Make a large loop by tying a loose knot in the middle of the bandage or cloth.
2. Hold the ends up, one in each hand.
3. Slip the loop over the dog's muzzle and lower jaw, just behind his nose.

A good way to prevent sunburn is to put a T-shirt on your Doberman Pinscher. Owner, Sheila Bonas.

Due to their short coats and low body fat, Doberman Pinschers can suffer from frostbite if they are left outside in the cold weather for a prolonged period of time. It is probably time for this Dobe to come inside and warm up. Owner, Beth Bishop.

4. Quickly tighten the loop so he can't open his mouth.
5. Tie the ends under his lower jaw.
6. Make a knot there and pull the ends back on each side of his face, under the ears, to the back of his head.

If he should start to vomit, you will need to remove the muzzle immediately. Otherwise, he could aspirate vomitus into his lungs.

ANTIFREEZE POISONING

Antifreeze in the driveway is a potential killer. Because antifreeze is sweet, dogs will lap it up. The active ingredient in antifreeze is ethylene glycol, which causes irreversible kidney damage. If you witness your pet ingesting antifreeze, you should call your veterinarian immediately. He may recommend that you induce vomiting at once by using hydrogen peroxide, or he may recommend a test to confirm antifreeze ingestion. Treatment is aggressive and must be administered promptly if the dog is to live, but you wouldn't want to subject your dog to unnecessary treatment.

BEE STINGS

A severe reaction to a bee sting (anaphylaxis) can result in difficulty breathing, collapse and even death. A symptom of a bee sting is swelling around the muzzle and face. Bee stings are antihistamine responsive. Over-the-counter antihistamines are available. Ask your veterinarian for recommendations on safe antihistamines to use and doses to administer. You should monitor the dog's gum color and respirations and watch for a decrease in swelling. If your dog is showing signs of anaphylaxis, your veterinarian may need to give him an injection of corticosteroids. It would be wise to call your veterinarian and confirm treatment.

BLEEDING

Bleeding can occur in many forms, such as a ripped dewclaw, a toenail cut too short, a puncture wound, a severe laceration, etc. If a pressure bandage is needed, it must be released every 15-20 minutes. Be careful of elastic bandages since it is easy to apply them too tightly. Any bandage material should be clean. If no regular bandage is available, a small towel or wash cloth can be used to cover the wound and bind it with a necktie, scarf, or something similar. Styptic powder, or even a soft cake of soap, can be used to stop a bleeding toenail. A ripped dewclaw or toenail may need to be cut back by the veterinarian and possibly treated with antibiotics. Depending on their severity, lacerations and puncture wounds may also need professional treatment. Your first thought should be to clean the wound with peroxide, soap and water, or some other antiseptic cleanser. Don't use alcohol since it deters the healing of the tissue.

BLOAT

Although not generally considered a first aid situation, bloat can occur in a dog rather suddenly. Truly, it is an emergency! Gastric dilatation-volvulus or gastric torsion—the twisting of the stomach to cut off both entry and exit, causing the organ to "bloat," is a disorder primarily found in the larger, more deep-chested breeds. It is life threatening and requires immediate veterinary assistance.

BURNS

If your dog gets a chemical burn, call your veterinarian immediately. Rinse any other burns with cold water and if the burn is significant, call your veterinarian. It may be necessary to clip the hair around the burn so it will be easier to keep clean. You can cleanse the wound on a daily basis with saline and apply a topical antimicrobial ointment, such as silver sulfadiazine 1 percent cream or gentamicin cream. Burns can be debilitating, especially to an older pet. They can cause pain and shock. It takes about three weeks for the skin to slough after the burn and there is the possibility of permanent hair loss.

CARDIOPULMONARY RESUSCITATION (CPR)

Check to see if your dog has a heart beat, pulse and spontaneous respiration. If his pupils are already dilated and fixed, the prognosis is less favorable. This is an emergency situation that requires two people to administer lifesaving techniques. One person needs to breathe for the dog while the other person tries to establish heart rhythm. Mouth to mouth resuscitation starts with two initial breaths, one to one and a half seconds in duration. After the initial breaths, breathe for the dog once after every five chest compressions. (You do not want to expand the dog's lungs while his chest is being compressed.) You inhale, cover the dog's nose with your mouth, and exhale *gently*. You should see the dog's chest expand. Sometimes, pulling the tongue forward stimulates respiration. You should be ventilating the dog 12-20 times per minute. The person managing the chest compressions should have the dog lying on his right side with one hand on either side of the dog's chest, directed over the heart between the fourth and fifth ribs (usually this is the point of the flexed elbow). The number of compressions administered depends on the size of the patient. Attempt 80-120 compressions per minute. Check for spontaneous respiration and/or heart beat. If present, monitor the patient and discontinue resuscitation. If you haven't already done so, call your veterinarian at once and make arrangements to take your pet in for professional treatment.

CHOCOLATE TOXICOSIS

Dogs like chocolate, but chocolate kills dogs. Its two basic chemicals, caffeine and theobromine, overstimulate the dog's nervous system. Ten ounces of milk chocolate can kill a 12-pound dog. Symptoms of poisoning include restlessness, vomiting, increased heart rate, seizure, and coma. Death is possible. If your dog has ingested chocolate, you can give syrup of ipecac at a dosage of one-eighth of a teaspoon per pound to induce vomiting. Two tablespoons of hydrogen peroxide is an alternative treatment.

While interaction with other dogs is important, supervision is always vital. Should a fight ensue, you must be able to intervene, bearing in mind the safety of the dog and yourself. Owner, Christine Filler.

By offering your Doberman safe chew toys, such as products made by Nylabone®, you will lessen his risk of choking.

CHOKING

You need to open the dog's mouth to see if any object is visible. Try to hold him upside down to see if the object can be dislodged. While you are working on your dog, call your veterinarian, as time may be critical.

DOG BITES

If your dog is bitten, wash the area and determine the severity of the situation. Some bites may need immediate attention, for instance, if it is bleeding profusely or if a lung is punctured. Other bites may be only superficial scrapes. Most dog bite cases need to be seen by the veterinarian, and some may require antibiotics. It is important that you learn if the offending dog has had a rabies vaccination. This is important for your dog, but also for you, in case you are the victim. Wash the wound and call your doctor for further instructions. You should check on your tetanus vaccination history. Rarely, and I mean rarely, do dogs get tetanus. If the offending dog is a stray, try to confine him for observation. He will need to be confined for ten days. A dog that has bitten a human and is not current on his rabies vaccination cannot receive a rabies vaccination for ten days. Dog bites should be reported to the Board of Health.

DROWNING

Remove any debris from the dog's mouth and swing the dog,

Always supervise your Doberman Pinscher when in a swimming pool and make sure that he knows how to get out.

holding him upside down. Stimulate respiration by pulling his tongue forward. Administer CPR if necessary, and call your veterinarian. Don't give up working on the dog. Be sure to wrap him in blankets if he is cold or in shock.

ELECTROCUTION

You may want to look into puppy proofing your house by installing GFCIs (Ground Fault Circuit Interrupters) on your electrical outlets. A GFCI just saved my dog's life. He had pulled an extension cord into his crate and was "teething" on it at seven years of age. The GFCI kept him from being electrocuted. Turn off the current before touching the dog. Resusci-

tate him by administering CPR and pulling his tongue forward to stimulate respiration. Try mouth-to-mouth breathing if the dog is not breathing. Take him to your veterinarian as soon as possible since electrocution can cause internal problems, such as lung damage, which need medical treatment.

EYES

Red eyes indicate inflammation, and any redness to the upper white part of the eye (sclera) may constitute an emergency. Squinting, cloudiness to the cornea, or loss of vision could indicate severe problems, such as glaucoma, anterior uveitis and episcleritis. Glaucoma is an emergency if you want to save the dog's eye. A prolapsed third eyelid is abnormal and is a symptom of an underlying problem. If something should get in your dog's eye, flush it out with cold water or a saline eye wash. Epiphora and allergic conjunctivitis are annoying and frequently persistent problems. Epiphora (excessive tearing) leaves the area below the eye wet and sometimes stained. The wetness may lead to a bacterial infection. There are numerous causes (allergies, infections, foreign matter, abnormally located eyelashes and adjacent facial hair that rubs against the eyeball, defects or diseases of the tear drainage system, birth defects of the eyelids, etc.) and the treatment is based on the cause. Keeping the hair around the eye cut short and sponging the eye daily will give relief. Many cases are responsive to medical treatment. Allergic conjunctivitis may be a seasonal problem if the dog has inhalant allergies (e.g., ragweed), or it may be a year 'round problem. The conjunctiva becomes red and swollen and is prone to a bacterial infection associated with mucus accumulation or pus in the eye. Again keeping the hair around the eyes short will give relief. Mild corti-costeroid drops or ointment will also give relief. The underlying problem should be investigated.

FISH HOOKS

An imbedded fish hook will probably need to be removed by the veterinarian. More than likely, sedation will be required along with antibiotics. Don't try to remove it yourself. The shank of the hook will need to be cut off in order to push the other end through.

FOREIGN OBJECTS

I can't tell you how many chicken bones my first dog ingested. Fortunately she had a "cast iron stomach" and never

Recreational swimming is ideal exercise for the Doberman Pinscher, especially in the summer months. Be aware of potential dangers in any river or lake in which you allow your dog to swim.

suffered the consequences. However, she was always going to the veterinarian for treatment. Not all dogs are so lucky. It is unbelievable what some dogs will take a liking to. I have assisted in surgeries in which all kinds of foreign objects were removed from the stomach and/or intestinal tract. Those objects included socks, pantyhose, stockings, clothing, diapers, sanitary products, plastic, toys, and, last but not least, rawhides. Surgery is costly and not always successful, especially if it is performed too late. If you see or suspect your dog has ingested a foreign object, contact your veterinarian immediately. He may tell you to induce vomiting or he may have you bring your dog to the clinic immediately. Don't induce vomiting without the veterinarian's permission, since the object may cause more damage on the way back up than it would if you allow it to pass through.

HEATSTROKE

Heatstroke is an emergency! The classic signs are rapid, shallow breathing; rapid heartbeat; a temperature above 104 degrees; and subsequent collapse. The dog needs to be cooled as quickly as possible and treated immediately by the veterinar-

ian. If possible, spray him down with cool water and pack ice around his head, neck, and groin. Monitor his temperature and stop the cooling process as soon as his temperature reaches 103 degrees. Nevertheless, you will need to keep monitoring his temperature to be sure it doesn't elevate again. If the temperature continues to drop to below 100 degrees, it could be life threatening. Get professional help immediately. Prevention is more successful than treatment. Those at the greatest risk are brachycephalic (short nosed) breeds, obese dogs, and those that suffer from cardiovascular disease. Dogs are not able to cool off by sweating as people can. Their only way is through panting and radiation of heat from the skin surface. When stressed and exposed to high environmental temperature, high humidity, and poor ventilation, a dog can suffer heatstroke very quickly. Many people do not realize how quickly a car can overheat. Never leave a dog unattended in a car. It is even against the law in some states. Also, a brachycephalic, obese, or infirm dog should never be left unattended outside during inclement weather and should have his activities curtailed. Any dog left outside, by law, must be assured adequate shelter (including shade) and fresh water.

POISONS

Try to locate the source of the poison (the container which lists the ingredients) and call your veterinarian immediately. Be prepared to give the age and weight of your dog, the quantity of poison consumed and the probable time of ingestion. Your veterinarian will want you to read off the ingredients. If you can't reach him, you can call a local poison center or the National Poison Control Center for Animals in Illinois, which is open 24 hours a day. Their phone number is 1-800-548-2423. There is a charge for their service, so you may need to have a credit card number available.

Symptoms of poisoning include muscle trembling and weakness, increased salivation, vomiting and loss of bowel control. There are numerous household toxins (over 500,000). A dog can be poisoned by toxins in the garbage. Other poisons include pesticides, pain relievers, prescription drugs, plants, chocolate, and cleansers. Since I own small dogs I don't have to worry about my dogs jumping up to the kitchen counters, but when I owned a large breed she would clean the counter, eating all the prescription medications.

Your pet can be poisoned by means other than directly ingesting the toxin. Ingesting a rodent that has ingested a rodenticide is one example. It is possible for a dog to have a reaction to the pesticides used by exterminators. If this is suspected you should contact the exterminator about the potential dangers of the pesticides used and their side effects.

Don't give human drugs to your dog unless your veterinar-

There are many plants and flowers that are poisonous to dogs. It is best to know which plants are toxic and keep your Doberman away from them.

ian has given his approval. Some human medications can be deadly to dogs.

This list was published in the American Kennel Club *Gazette*, February, 1995. As the list states these are common poisonous

POISONOUS PLANTS

Amaryllis (bulb)	Jasmine (berries)
Andromeda	Jerusalem Cherry
Apple Seeds (cyanide)	Jimson Weed
Arrowgrass	Laburnum
Avocado	Larkspur
Azalea	Laurel
Bittersweet	Locoweed
Boxwood	Marigold
Buttercup	Marijuana
Caladium	Mistletoe (berries)
Castor Bean	Monkshood
Cherry Pits	Mushrooms
Chokecherry	Narcissus (bulb)
Climbing Lily	Nightshade
Crown of Thorns	Oleander
Daffodil (bulb)	Peach
Daphne	Philodendron
Delphinium	Poison Ivy
Dieffenbachia	Privet
Dumb Cane	Rhododendron
Elderberry	Rhubarb
Elephant Ear	Snow on
English Ivy	the Mountain
Foxglove	Stinging Nettle
Hemlock	Toadstool
Holly	Tobacco
Hyacinth (bulb)	Tulip (bulb)
Hydrangea	Walnut
Iris (bulb)	Wisteria
Japanese Yew	Yew

plants, but this list may not be complete. If your dog ingests a poisonous plant, try to identify it and call your veterinarian. Some plants cause more harm than others.

PORCUPINE QUILLS

Removal of quills is best left up to your veterinarian since it can be quite painful. Your unhappy dog would probably appreciate being sedated for the removal of the quills.

SEIZURE (CONVULSION OR FIT)

Many breeds, including mixed breeds, are predisposed to seizures, although a seizure may be secondary to an underlying medical condition. Usually a seizure is not considered an emergency unless it lasts longer than ten minutes. Nevertheless, you should notify your veterinarian. Dogs do not swallow their tongues. Do not handle the dog's mouth since your dog probably cannot control his actions and may inadvertently bite you. The seizure can be mild; for instance, a dog can have a seizure standing up. More frequently the dog will lose consciousness and may urinate and/or defecate. The best thing you can do for your dog is to put him in a safe place or to block off the stairs or areas where he can fall.

SEVERE TRAUMA

See that the dog's head and neck are extended so if the dog is unconscious or in shock, he is able to breathe. If there is any vomitus, you should try to get the head extended down with the body elevated to prevent

Your Doberman Pinscher depends on you for love and care. Knowing first aid can help to save his life one day.

vomitus from being aspirated. Alert your veterinarian that you are on your way.

SHOCK

Shock is a life threatening condition and requires immediate veterinary care. It can occur after an injury or even after severe fright. Other causes of shock are hemorrhage, fluid loss, sepsis, toxins, adrenal insufficiency, cardiac failure, and anaphylaxis. The symptoms are a rapid weak pulse, shallow breathing, dilated pupils, subnormal temperature, and muscle weakness. The capillary refill time (CRT) is slow, taking longer than two seconds for normal gum color to return. Keep the dog warm while transporting him to the veterinary clinic. Time is critical for survival.

SKUNKS

Skunk spraying is not necessarily an emergency, although it would be in my house. If the dog's eyes are sprayed, you need to rinse them well with water. One remedy for deskunking the dog is to wash him in tomato juice and follow with a soap and water bath. The newest remedy is bathing the dog in a mixture of one quart of three percent hydrogen peroxide, quarter cup baking soda, and one teaspoon liquid soap. Rinse well. There are also commercial products available.

SNAKE BITES

It is always a good idea to know what poisonous snakes reside in your area. Rattlesnakes, water moccasins, copperheads, and coral snakes are residents of some areas of the United States. Pack ice around the area that is bitten and call your veterinarian immediately to alert him that you are on your way. Try to identify the snake or at least be able to describe it (for the use of antivenin). It is possible that he may send you to another clinic that has the proper antivenin.

TOAD POISONING

Bufo toads are quite deadly. You should find out if these nasty little critters are native to your area.

VACCINATION REACTION

Once in a while, a dog may suffer an anaphylactic reaction to a vaccine. Symptoms include swelling around the muzzle, extending to the eyes. Your veterinarian may ask you to return to his office to determine the severity of the reaction. It is possible that your dog may need to stay at the hospital for a few hours during future vaccinations.

RECOMMENDED READING

DR. ACKERMAN'S DOG BOOKS FROM T.F.H.

OWNER'S GUIDE TO DOG HEALTH

TS-214, 432 pages
Over 300 color photographs

Winner of the 1995 Dog Writers Association of America's Best Health Book, this comprehensive title gives accurate, up-to-date information on all the major disorders and conditions found in dogs. Completely illustrated to help owners visualize signs of illness, different states of infection, procedures and treatment, it covers nutrition, skin disorders, disorders of the major body systems (reproductive, digestive, respiratory), eye problems, vaccines and vaccinations, dental health and more.

SKIN & COAT CARE FOR YOUR DOG

TS-249, 224 pages
Over 200 color photographs

Dr. Ackerman, a specialist in the field of dermatology and a Diplomate of the American College of Veterinary Dermatology, joins 14 of the world's most respected dermatologists and other experts to produce an extremely helpful manual on the dog's skin. Coat and skin problems are extremely common in the dog, and owners need to better understand the conditions that affect their dogs' coats. The book details everything from the basics of parasites and mange to grooming techniques, medications, hair loss and more.

DOG BEHAVIOR AND TRAINING
Veterinary Advice for Owners

TS-252, 292 pages
Over 200 color photographs

Joined by co-editors Gary Landsberg, DVM and Wayne Hunthausen, DVM, Dr. Ackerman and about 20 experts in behavioral studies and training set forth a practical guide to the common problems owners experience with their dogs. Since behavioral disorders are the number-one reason for owners to abandon a dog, it is essential for owners to understand how the dog thinks and how to correct him if he misbehaves. The book covers socialization, selection, rewards and punishment, puppy-problem prevention, excitable and disobedient behaviors, sexual behaviors, aggression, children, stress and more.

RECOMMENDED READING
OTHER DOBERMAN PINSCHER BOOKS FROM T.F.H.

THE WORLD OF DOBERMAN PINSCHERS
by Anna Katherine Nicholas

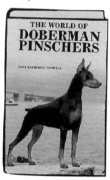

H-1082, 640 pages
Over 800 full-color photos
The World of the Doberman Pinscher is the largest, most complete, and most authoritative work ever created on the breed, having been written by one of the world's most respected dog show judges, Anna Katherine Nicholas. Hundreds of fascinating photographs beautifully enhance an eminently readable text. Aside from the book's aesthetic appeal, there is value for all who read it: practical value for first-time Doberman owners and novices, historical value for show enthusiasts and breeders, and sentimental value for veteran Dobe fanciers.

THE DOBERMAN PINSCHER
by Woodrow Kerfmann

PS-808, 256 pages
Color &b/w photographs
The Doberman Pinscher concentrates on providing the type of sound practical advice that is of special benefit to first-time owners of the breed, but it also contains more than enough information to make it valuable to long-time fanciers as well. Illustrated throughout with beautiful photos, the book presents a wide-ranging gallery of pictorial tributes to past and present representatives of the breed.

THE BOOK OF THE DOBERMAN PINSCHER
by Joan McDonald Brearley

H-968, 576 pages
Color & b/w photographs
In *The Book of the Doberman Pinscher*, author Joan McDonald Brearley has compiled a most interesting, comprehensive, and timely account of the Doberman Pinscher, covering all aspects of the breed from transport to America to war involvement, breeding and general care. Included also are a Dictionary of Dog Diseases and a Glossary of Dog Terms. To complement the text, hundreds of photos are included of great historic dogs as well as charming candid at-home photos and show poses.